How Nations Escape Poverty

"Read this brilliant, highly readable, inspiring book before the woke cancel culture hears about it! The astonishing tales told here about the miraculous transformation of two seemingly disparate nations—Poland and Vietnam— from socialist sinkholes of misery into vibrant, prosperous, opportunity-rich economies resoundingly reaffirm the truth of the positive, inclusive power of free markets. This book couldn't be more timely in today's troubled world."
Steve Forbes, editor-in-chief, *Forbes*

"Many great libertarian thinkers were economists or philosophers. Zitelmann is a historian and sociologist. He does not argue theoretically, but empirically. In his book, he shows that development aid and redistribution do not eliminate poverty, but private property, entrepreneurship, and capitalism do."
John Mackey, co-founder, Whole Foods Markets

"Anti-capitalists believe that the economy is a zero-sum game. They want to help the poor by taking money away from the rich. They want to help poor countries through development aid. Based on scientific studies, Zitelmann shows that this concept has never worked. But as soon as people are given more economic freedom, their standard of living improves dramatically, as Zitelmann demonstrates through the examples of Poland and Vietnam. Capitalism is so effective that even a few drops of it can work wonders. What miracles would only be possible with real capitalism?"
Jennifer Grossman, CEO, Atlas Society

"Public intellectuals in relatively free economies have crippled poor nations struggling to rebuild after years of socialism by lying to the world about how jobs and wealth are created. A powerful and needed antidote to the lies of the self-hating academics is Dr. Rainer Zitelmann's new book examining and highlighting the success of Poland and Vietnam emerging from imposed economic statism. The model that built the modern West can also rebuild those nations enslaved during the Cold War: property rights, low tax and regulatory regimes, open trade and limited government."
Grover Norquist, president of Americans for Tax Reform

"One of the most exciting developments over the last quarter-century has been the revival of social and economic freedom in both Eastern Europe and Asia. Zitelmann's case studies show how they did it, and what other countries need to do to enjoy a similar revival."
Eamonn Butler, director, the Adam Smith Institute, London

"Imparting surprises on every page, even for sophisticated theorists of capitalism, Zitelmann's book makes a major new contribution to the wealth of nations."

George Gilder, author of *Wealth and Poverty*

"This book reminds us with unimpeachable data that economic freedom is the key to prosperity and socialism is the best path to despair. The paradox is why so many young people are taught and believe exactly the opposite. We might as well be teaching them that the sun rises in the west and sets in the east."

Stephen Moore, senior economist, The Heritage Foundation

"Rainer Zitelmann has been one of the most prolific and effective defenders of free enterprise for many years. In his new book, Zitelmann details the political and economic reforms that turned once poor and stagnating communist basket cases of Vietnam and Poland into fast-growing economies whose people enjoy much improved standards of living. It should be read by would-be reformers everywhere."

Marian Tupy, senior fellow, the Cato Institute, and founder of HumanProgress.org

"Capitalism has lacked a unifying public figure since Milton Friedman left the building in 2006. Now, there is, at long last, a worthy candidate for Friedman's rightful successor. I praise Dr. Rainer Zitelmann as the reigning public intellectual champion of capitalism. With his book *How Nations Escape Poverty*, he proves once again that as a historian and sociologist he has followed in the footsteps of the greatest freedom thinkers."

Ralph Benko, co-author of *The Capitalist Manifesto* and co-founder and chairman of the Capitalist League

"Billionaires usually get a bad press, but Rainer Zitelmann shows in his outstanding new book that economic growth takes off when free markets permit them to create new products and encourage other people to emulate them. As Adam Smith long ago argued, economic growth is the key to ending poverty. Zitelmann documents his thesis to the hilt through detailed accounts of the economies of Poland and Vietnam. The book is a magnificent achievement."

David Gordon, senior fellow, Ludwig von Mises Institute, and editor of the *Journal of Libertarian Studies*

How Nations Escape Poverty

Vietnam, Poland, and the Origins of Prosperity

RAINER ZITELMANN

Encounter
BOOKS

New York • London

First American edition published in 2024 by Encounter Books,
an activity of Encounter for Culture and Education, Inc.,
a nonprofit, tax-exempt corporation.
Encounter Books website address: www.encounterbooks.com

Manufactured in the United States and printed on
acid-free paper. The paper used in this publication meets
the minimum requirements of ANSI/NISO Z39.48–1992
(R 1997) (*Permanence of Paper*).

FIRST AMERICAN EDITION

LIBRARY OF CONGRESS CATALOGING-IN-PUBLICATION DATA IS AVAILABLE

Information for this title can be found at the Library of Congress
website under the following ISBN 978-1-64177-395-9 and LCCN 2024001954.

CONTENTS

FOREWORD

The Dazzling Dozen: Rainer's Rules of Wealth and Poverty

Rainer Zitelmann is a supreme entrepreneurial historian and philosopher, ingenious pollster, and practitioner of the arts and enigmas of the wealth and poverty of nations. A remorseless seeker of facts rather than self-serving myths, he scrupulously documents his shocking revelations with detailed and authoritative data.

His iconoclastic views can be summed up in twelve key epiphanies.

1. Key to economic growth and enterprise is admiration and emulation of the rich. Key to poverty and sloth is demoralization of the poor by telling them they are victims of the rich.
2. Poverty stems from envy and resentment toward wealth as a zero-sum game. Wealth stems from the desire and freedom to become rich in ever-expanding circles of gain. Vietnamese and Polish citizens now harbor more favorable attitudes toward the rich than do Americans or Germans. Thus, the Vietnamese and Polish economies have grown far faster than apparently privileged Western rivals. An explanation: Zitelmann's polls show that staunch Marxist views are far more common in so-called

"capitalist" US or Europe than in so-called "communist" parts of Asia, such as Vietnam.

3. Fifty years and trillions of dollars of development aid and 100 years of socialist giveaways prove that the prime cause of poverty among nations is government redistribution of wealth. The chief source of new wealth and growth is entrepreneurial disruption of incumbent wealth.

4. Around the globe, the more "aid" the less growth. Scrutiny of hundreds of studies shows that economic growth and escape from poverty are inversely proportional to the amount of development aid received. Foreign aid goes to governments and trickles down only to bureaucrats and "crony capitalists," not to the people.

5. Inequality always rises as people escape poverty. Suppress inequality and growth stalls.

6. Enterprise, unlike socialism, cannot be decreed from the top down; it must be freed from the bottom up.

7. Rapid reformers experience shorter recessions and quicker recoveries and attract far more foreign investment than do gradualist reformers.

8. Support for capitalism in polls rises in proportion to the avoidance of using the term. Westerners should stress dynamism and freedom rather than "capitalist" wealth.

9. The fatal flaw of current democracies is giving incumbent governments and their central banks the power to print money to finance their friends and frivols, buy off voters with redistribution schemes, and disguise failure with flamboyant demagoguery and giveaways. In a portentous lesson for the West, Argentina and Venezuela were both among the richest countries in the world, but they gave it all up pursuing demagogic class warfare and socialism under Juan Perón and Hugo Chávez.

10. Zitelmann's bikini law of accounting transparency and truth eclipsing concealment and complexity: *less is more.* Example: Nguyen Thi Phuong-Thao (the one woman among seven Vietnamese billionaires) went from selling fax machines as a student in Moscow in 1981 to launching a low-cost airline, VietJet Air. Saving money on uniforms and delighting customers, she encouraged her steward-esses to wear bikinis, which, she points out boldly, "shows beautiful characteristics" and "makes people happy." The same applies to accounting.

11. Zitelmann's Law of Corruption: *more is more.* The more influence a government has over a country, the more pervasive is corruption; the more interventions by bureau-crats, the more chances to bribe them.

12. Zitelmann's final Polish joke: Poland beating out the rest of Europe and America in economic growth since the 1989 emancipation of Polish enterprise, with more than one million new private firms launched in four years and per capita GDP up 2.5 times by 2017.

The information theory behind the huge growth of the global information economy (and my *Life After Capitalism*) identifies wealth as knowledge, growth as learning, money as tokenized time, and new knowledge as "surprisal." In information theory, information is "unexpected bits." Imparting surprises on every page, even for sophisticated theorists of capitalism, Zitelmann's book makes a major new contribution to the wealth of nations.

George Gilder, author of *Wealth & Poverty* (1980)
and *Life After Capitalism* (2023)

PREFACE

I have written several books on wealth, so why am I now writing a book on poverty? Because, as a result of my research, I have come to the apparently paradoxical conclusion that only a society that allows people to become rich and have a positive attitude toward wealth can overcome poverty.

Representative opinion polls that I have commissioned in numerous countries have revealed that there are two countries in particular in which people have a positive attitude toward wealth and the rich: Poland and Vietnam. At the same time, these are also two countries in which people (despite the different political systems) have a more positive view of the term 'capitalism' than their peers in most other countries.

And these are two countries that have made extraordinary gains in economic freedom over the past few decades. The Heritage Foundation has been publishing its *Index of Economic Freedom* (you could also call it a capitalism index) every year since 1995, and in no countries of comparable size has economic freedom increased as much during that time as in Poland and Vietnam.

There is more that unites these two countries than economic success: Both experienced terrible wars in which many millions of people lost their lives—the Second World War in Poland, and the Indochina War in Vietnam. After the wars ended, socialist planned economies were established in both countries, destroying what the war had not already devastated. As a result, Vietnam became one of the poorest countries in the world and Poland one of the poorest countries in Europe. In this book, I describe life in these countries under a planned economy and reveal how bitterly poor the majority of people in these two countries were.

The Vietnamese initiated a program of market-economy reforms in 1986, called *Doi Moi* ("innovation" or "renovation" in English). A few years later, Poland also decided to implement market-economy reforms. In both countries, these reforms led to remarkable economic growth and dramatic improvements in living standards. I will illustrate this by using figures and statistics, as well as by drawing on the accounts of Polish and Vietnamese individuals.

This book begins with a chapter in which I explain the continued relevance of Adam Smith's ideas, which showed that only economic freedom can defeat poverty. I then describe what *does not* help overcome poverty, namely development aid. From there, I analyze how capitalism has helped people in Vietnam and Poland to improve their standards of living and escape the clutches of poverty. I think many other countries stand to learn a great deal from the experiences of these two countries.

I thank all of my friends in Vietnam and Poland who helped me with this book. Le Chi Mai from Hanoi handled translations and conducted interviews for me, and I thank Nguyen Quoc Minh-Quang, Vu Dinh Loc, Nguyen Trong Hoa, Lam Duc Hung, and Nguyen Thi Quat for the interviews they gave. I would also like to thank the attorney Dr. Oliver Massmann, who has been working in Hanoi for twenty-five years and was instrumental in the formulation of the US-Vietnam Free Trade Agreement, for the details he provided. And Dinh Tuan Minh, a representative of a market-economy think-tank, who explained some important things to me during a conversation in Hanoi. I am particularly grateful to Professor Andreas Stoffers, the head of the Friedrich Naumann Foundation in Vietnam, who provided me with numerous contacts.

In Poland, my publisher Krzysztof Zuber (Wydawnictwo Freedom Publishing) and my advisor Marcin Chmielowski helped me immensely—thank you for that! I would also like to thank the former Minister of Finance of Poland, Professor Leszek Balcerowicz, whose reforms were a major reason behind Poland's economic recovery and rise. In addition, I want to thank Marcin Zieliński (Forum Obywatelskiego Rozwoju), Marek Tatała (Fundacja Wolności Gospodarczej), Mateusz Machaj (Instytut Edukacji Ekonomicznej im. Ludwiga von Misesa), Alicja Wancerz-Gluza (co-founder of the Karta Center) and Tomasz Agencki, with whom I produced the film *Poland: From Socialism to Prosperity*.

I would also like to thank Ansgar Graw, who did an excellent job editing the book, and Sebastian Taylor, who translated it into English.

I admire the people in Poland and Vietnam, and I also have something very personal in common with them: because the two longest and most important relationships in my life were with Monika, whose parents came from Poland, and Trang, whose parents are from Vietnam.

Dr. Rainer Zitelmann, December 2023

CHAPTER ONE

ADAM SMITH WAS RIGHT: ONLY ECONOMIC FREEDOM CAN DEFEAT POVERTY

We know very little about the man Adam Smith. We do not even know the famous Scotsman's birthday. All we know is the date of his baptism, June 5, 1723 (Julian calendar), which means that, according to our Gregorian calendar, he was baptized on June 16. He never knew his father, a customs official, who died at the age of forty-four just a few months before Adam Smith was born.

The most important person in his life was his mother, who not only raised him, but with whom he lived until her death in 1784. Smith never married. We only know that he fell in love twice, but his feelings were not reciprocated, which may have been due to the fact that he was considered rather unattractive. At the age of seventeen, he began six years of study at Oxford, but wasn't impressed by the university. He later spoke disparagingly of his professors, whom he considered lazy. Before the age of thirty, he was appointed professor of moral philosophy at Glasgow University and published his first major work, *The Theory of Moral Sentiments*. He published only two major works in his entire life, with *The Wealth of Nations*, published in 1776, being by far the better known. He wrote more books, but he had the manuscripts burned before his death, so we are left with only these two books and a number of his essays and transcripts of his lectures.

Among those who have never read Smith's books, he is sometimes seen as a proponent of extreme selfishness, even, perhaps, as the spiritual father of the Gordon Gekko–style rapacious capitalist who exclaims "Greed is good!" in the movie *Wall Street*. However, this is a distorted image that stems from the fact that Smith strongly emphasized the self-interest of economic subjects in his book *The Wealth of Nations*. But this picture is most definitely a misrepresentation.

The first chapter of his book *The Theory of Moral Sentiments* begins with a section "Of Sympathy," in which he defined sympathy as "fellow-feeling with any passion whatsoever."[1] Today we would probably use the word "empathy": "How selfish soever man may be supposed, there are evidently some principles in his nature, which interest him in the fortunes of others, and render their happiness necessary to him, though he derives nothing from it, except the pleasure of seeing it. Of this kind is pity or compassion, the emotion we feel for the misery of others, when we either see it, or are made to conceive it in a very lively manner."[2]

Adam Smith's sympathy was especially for the poor. He drew income from various sources that added up to 900 pounds a year, which was three to four times the salary of a university professor.[3] But when Smith's last will and testament was read, it left his nephew David Douglas feeling distinctly disappointed. He received far less than he had hoped for. The will confirmed what Smith's friends had long suspected: Smith had donated almost his entire fortune to the poor, mostly in secret. His generosity had, in fact, even resulted in Smith getting into money trouble himself at one point.[4]

If you read his two main works, *The Wealth of Nations* and *The Theory of Moral Sentiments*, you will be hard pressed to find a single passage where he speaks positively about the rich and powerful. Merchants and landlords are almost exclusively painted in a negative light, primarily as people who want to assert their selfish interests and who strive to create monopolies. "Our merchants and master-manufacturers complain of the bad effects of high wages in raising the price, and thereby lessening the sale of their goods both at home and abroad. They say nothing concerning the bad effects of high profits. They are silent with regard to the pernicious effects of their own gains. They complain only of those of other people."[5] Or: "People of the same trade seldom meet together, even for merriment and diversion, but the conversation ends in a conspiracy against the public, or in some contrivance to raise prices."[6]

There are more positive sentences about capitalists in Marx and Engels's *Communist Manifesto* than anywhere in the works of Adam Smith. The bourgeoisie constantly create more powerful forces of production than all past generations combined, Marx and Engels write with admiration. There is no trace of such admiration in Smith's work; instead, the rich are the target of caustic criticism. Defenders of Smith argue that this does not reflect any kind of general resentment against entrepreneurs or the rich, but rather Smith's advocacy of free competition and opposition to monopolies. That is certainly one aspect, but still, reading his two major works, one gets the impression that, ultimately, Smith dislikes the rich as much as he dislikes politicians. Even Adam Smith was not free of the resentment traditionally harbored by intellectuals against the rich.[7]

Conversely, however, there are many passages that exhibit sympathy for the condition of the "poor," whereby Smith did not restrict himself to the poor in the strictest sense of the word, but included the "not rich," "that is, the condition of the vast majority of the population who must exchange labor for wages in order to earn a living."[8] In *Adam Smith's America*, Glory M. Liu documents the enduring fascination with Adam Smith and presents an overview of the latest Smith-related research: "There is an almost unanimous agreement that, for Smith, the most important feature of commercial society was that it improved the condition of the poor."[9]

There is a famous passage from *The Wealth of Nations*: "No society can surely be flourishing and happy, of which the far greater part of the members are poor and miserable. It is but equity, besides, that they who feed, clothe, and lodge the whole body of the people, should have such a share of the produce of so much of their own labor as to be themselves tolerably well fed, clothed, and lodged."[10]

Today, these words are sometimes misinterpreted to claim that Smith advocated government-led redistribution of wealth. That was not his intention and he was certainly not calling for social revolution. But poverty, according to Smith, was not pre-ordained. Above all, though, he did not trust governments. In Chapter Eight of *The Wealth of Nations*, along with the sentences quoted above, he points out that the only way to raise living standards is via economic growth.

Continuous economic growth is the only way to raise wages; a stagnant economy leads to falling wages. In another chapter, he writes that "famine has never arisen from any other cause but the violence of government attempting, by improper means, to remedy the inconveniences of a dearth."[11] How right he was is something we know full well 250 years later, after hundreds, if not thousands, of failed attempts to control inflation with price controls.

The "liberal reward of labour," Smith wrote, is "the effect of increasing wealth," and he repeatedly stressed that while "society is advancing to the further acquisition [...] the condition of the labouring poor, of the great body of the people, seems to be the happiest and the most comfortable. It is hard in the stationary, and miserable in the declining state."[12]

Karl Marx, on the other hand, believed he had discovered various economic "laws" that would necessarily lead to the downfall of capitalism, such as the "tendency of the rate of profit to fall" or the impoverishment of the proletariat. In his major work, *Capital*, Marx formulated this as follows:

> Along with the constantly diminishing number of the magnates of capital, who usurp and monopolise all advantages of this process of transformation, grows the mass of misery, oppression, slavery, degradation, exploitation; but with this too grows the revolt of the working class, a class always increasing in numbers, and disciplined, united, organised by the very mechanism of the process of capitalist production itself. The monopoly of capital becomes a fetter upon the mode of production, which has sprung up and flourished along with, and under it. Centralisation of the means of production and socialisation of labour at last reach a point where they become incompatible with their capitalist integument. This integument is burst asunder. The knell of capitalist private property sounds [...]. But capitalist production begets, with the inexorability of a law of Nature, its own negation.[13]

When *The Wealth of Nations* was published in 1776, capitalism was still in its infancy and the overwhelming majority of people lived in extreme poverty. And poverty meant something very different then than it does today. People were lean and small-boned; throughout history, the human body has adapted to inadequate caloric intake. "The small workers of the eighteenth century," Angus Deaton writes in his book *The Great Escape*, "were effectively locked into a nutritional trap; they could not earn much because they were so physically weak, and they could not eat enough because, without work, they did not have the money to buy food."[14]

Some people rave about the harmonious pre-capitalist conditions when life was so much slower, but this sluggishness was mainly a result of physical weakness due to permanent malnutrition.[15] It is estimated that 200 years ago, about 20 percent of the inhabitants of England and France were not able to work at all. As Johan Norberg explains in his book *Progress*, "At most they had enough energy for a few hours of slow walking per day, which condemned most of them to a life of begging."[16]

Smith predicted that only an expansion of markets could lead to increased prosperity, and this is precisely what has happened since the end of socialist planned economies. In China alone, the introduction of private property and market reforms have reduced the number of people living in extreme poverty from 88 percent in 1981 to less than 1 percent today. When I asked free-market economist Weiying Zhang of Peking University how relevant Smith was for China, he replied: "China's rapid economic development over the past four decades is a victory of Adam Smith's concept of the market." Contrary to prevailing interpretations in the West, economic growth and declining poverty in China was not "because of the state, but in spite of the state," explained Weiying Zhang, and was caused by the introduction of private property.

While Karl Marx believed that the condition of the poor could only be improved by abolishing private property, Smith believed in the power of the market. He was not an advocate of a libertarian utopia without the state; he believed that governments had important functions to fulfill. Nevertheless, in 1755, two decades before *The Wealth of Nations* appeared, he warned in a lecture:

Man is generally considered by statesmen and projectors as the materials of a sort of political mechanics. Projectors disturb nature in the course of her operations in human affairs; and it requires no more than to let her alone, and give her fair play in the pursuit of her ends, that she may establish her own designs [...]. All governments which thwart this natural course, which force things into another channel, or which endeavour to arrest the progress of society at a particular point, are unnatural, and to support themselves are obliged to be oppressive and tyrannical.[17]

These were indeed prophetic words. The biggest mistake planners have always made was clinging to the illusion that you can plan an economic order on paper. They believe that an author, sitting at a desk, can fashion an ideal economic order and that all that remains is to convince enough politicians to implement this new economic order in practice.

Friedrich August von Hayek later called this approach "constructivism," saying, "The idea of rational people sitting down together to consider how to remake the world is perhaps the most characteristic outcome of those design theories."[18] According to Hayek, the anti-rationalist insight into historical events that Smith shared with other Scottish Enlightenment thinkers such as David Hume and Adam Ferguson "enabled them for the first time to comprehend how institutions and morals, language and law, have evolved by a process of cumulative growth and that it is only with and within this framework that human reason has grown and can successfully operate."[19]

In the manner of an economic historian, Smith described economic development rather than outlining an ideal system.

Smith is often criticized today for highlighting the importance of self-interest. He emphasized the importance of selfishness precisely because people need help from other people all the time. However, he thought that people could not therefore rely solely on the goodwill of others. It is in this context, by the way, that Smith also employed the term "invisible hand," for which he became so famous, although this phrase appears only three times in his entire body of work. (This is similar to Joseph Schumpeter and the phrase "creative destruction," which he only ever used twice.)

> As every individual, therefore, endeavours as much as he can both to employ his capital in the support of domestic industry, and so to direct that industry that its produce may be of the greatest value; every individual necessarily labours to render the annual revenue of the society as great as he can. He generally, indeed, neither intends to promote the public interest, nor knows how much he is promoting it [...] and he is in this, as in many other cases, led by an invisible hand to promote an end which was no part of his intention. Nor is it always the worse for the society that it was no part of it. By pursuing his own interest he frequently promotes that of the society more effectually than when he really intends to promote it. I have never known much good done by those who affected to trade for the public good.[20]

The economist Ludwig von Mises emphasized that it is a mistake to contrast egoistic and altruistic actions. Fortunately, he explains, "The power to choose whether my actions and conduct shall serve myself or my fellow beings is not given to me [...]. If it were, human society would not be possible."[21] And Friedrich August von Hayek described as Adams Smith's greatest contribution to scientific thought (pointing far beyond economics) "his notion of a spontaneous order that creates complex structures like an invisible hand."[22]

But Smith's work has also been subjected to sharp criticism from within the circle of free-market economists. The libertarian American economist Murray N. Rothbard, in his monumental work *Economic Thought Before Adam Smith. An Austrian Perspec-*

tive on the History of Economic Thought, minces no words in his vilification of Smith, arguing that he was by no means the advocate of free-market economics that he is commonly portrayed as being. In fact, Rothbard alleges that Smith's erroneous labor theory of value makes him the forerunner of Karl Marx and claims that Marxists would certainly be justified in citing the Scottish philosopher and hailing him as the ultimate inspiration of their own founding father.[23] According to Rothbard, Smith failed to understand the economic function of the entrepreneur and even fell short of the insights provided by economists such as Richard Cantillon;[24] he supported state-imposed caps on the rate of interest, heavy taxes on luxurious consumption, and extensive government intervention in the economy.[25] On a personal level, Rothbard says Smith was also untrustworthy because he had previously campaigned for free trade but spent the final twelve years of his life as a commissioner of Scottish customs.[26]

Much of this criticism is certainly justified, and yet it would be wrong to call Adam Smith a left-winger. Even the American philosopher Samuel Fleischacker, who emphasizes Smith's leftist tendencies, concedes that Smith would not necessarily identify with contemporary social democrats or defend the modern welfare state.[27]

Against this criticism stand Smith's deep distrust of government intervention in the economy and his almost boundless faith in the "invisible hand" that steers markets in the right direction. When the economy is ruined, it is, according to Smith, never by entrepreneurs and merchants, but always by the state: "Great nations are never impoverished by private, though they sometimes are by public prodigality and misconduct," he wrote in *The Wealth of Nations.*[28] And he added optimistically: "The uniform, constant, and uninterrupted effort of every man to better his condition, the principle from which public and national, as well as private opulence is originally derived, is frequently powerful enough to maintain the natural progress of things toward improvement, in spite both of the extravagance of government and of the greatest errors of administration. Like the unknown principle of animal life, it frequently restores health and vigour to the constitution, in spite, not only of the disease, but of the absurd prescriptions of the doctor."[29]

The metaphor says a great deal: private economic actors represent healthy, positive development, while politicians obstruct the economy with their nonsensical regulations. Adam Smith would have been very skeptical today if he could see governments in Europe and the United States increasingly intervening in the economy and politicians who believe they are smarter than the market.

One of Smith's shortcomings was that he did not understand the economic function of the entrepreneur, which was later so brilliantly elaborated by thinkers such as Joseph Schumpeter. Erroneously, Smith saw the entrepreneur primarily as a manager and business leader rather than as an innovator. He recognized the importance of "empathy," but he did not equate it with entrepreneurship at any point in his work. Today, we see how Steve Jobs and other entrepreneurs have understood the needs and feelings of their customers better and earlier than the customers themselves, that empathy—and not "greed"—is indeed the basis of entrepreneurial success and the foundation of capitalism.

Smith's failure to understand the role of the entrepreneur and his evident resentment of the rich are indeed characteristics that he shares with those on the left of the political spectrum. However, this does not at all apply to his advocacy of improved conditions for workers. For, according to Smith, improving the situation of ordinary people would not come about through redistribution and excessive state intervention; it would be the natural result of economic growth, which in turn needed one thing above all: economic freedom. To the extent that economic freedom prevails and markets expand, people's standard of living will also rise. Three hundred years after Smith's birth and some 250 years after the publication of his *magnum opus*, we know that the moral philosopher and economist was right: private property and the market economy are the foundations of growth, and if the state does not interfere too much in the economy, everybody's lives will improve, especially those of the poor.

Proponents of capitalism have failed to place precisely these correlations at the heart of their defense of the market economy: it is not primarily the strong who need the market economy, because they will somehow manage in any system; it is the weak and the poor, whose only chance to improve their living conditions is in a free-market economy.

CHAPTER TWO

WHAT HELPS AGAINST POVERTY —AND WHAT DOESN'T

Frank Bremer has dedicated his life to the fight against poverty and has been involved in development aid in thirty countries across Africa, Central Asia, the Caribbean, and the Indian Ocean, preparing projects in the fields of rural development and the environment. After more than fifty years of involvement with development aid, he offers a scathing assessment: "Development aid is a project that carries out ineffective activities for an unachievable goal (poverty reduction) for a wrongly selected target group (African smallholder farmers) with a method that does not work (help for self-help) in an ineffective format (the project) which, like a flash in the pan, leaves no lasting traces on anyone involved apart from fond memories, uses most of the funds for project implementation, and thus takes what was originally a good idea and wastes a great deal of money."[1]

His judgement comes across as very harsh. I will go on to show, on the basis of objective research, what Bremer gets right and what is an exaggeration. To say it in advance: the fight against poverty remains one of the most important tasks facing humanity, but development aid (the politically correct word for this is now "development cooperation") is the wrong means to achieve this noble goal. In many cases, it has accomplished nothing. In others, it has actually achieved the very opposite of what was intended.

In his book *Fünfzig Jahre Entwicklungshilfe—Fünfzig Jahre Strohfeuer* [*Fifty Years of Development Aid—Fifty Years of Flash in the Pan*], Bremer reproduces a dialog between the head of a village community and a German development worker ("self-help expert"), which is fictional but made up of snippets of actual conversations and is based on Bremer's decades of practical experience in the field. Bremer had conducted the progress check for this project. I would like to quote the dialog in full: C is the head of the village community and S is the self-help expert.

C: "Sir, we need a small dam to provide water for our cattle and farmers in the dry season."

S: "That is a very sensible goal, but let me explain what you need first. You need to improve your management capacities to tackle a project like a dam; you need analytical tools, meetings and training on how to hold meetings and deal with group dynamics, as well as thinking about how to involve women; you need negotiation and decision-making techniques, which you can learn by consulting our experts, you need..."

C: "Oh sir, it seems as if that will all take a lot of time. If fresh water stays in the mouth too long, it turns into saliva. And our dam?"

S: "One step at a time, you need to be more process-oriented. Believe me, our self-help specialists know what you need to get your dam."

C: "Okay, once we've done all that, do we get our dam?"

S: "It is certainly possible. But before you tackle a big project like a dam, you should start small, e.g., digging a well by hand, without a pump and winch or anything."

C: "Sir, we have enough wells and boreholes, and some of them even have hand pumps. What we need is a dam."

S: "Ask the women in the village. I'm sure there are some who don't have a well yet."

C: "Okay, I guess beggars can't be choosers. We'll dig a well. Will we get a dam then?"

S: "That depends on you. Fifty-fifty participation in cash, plus provision of labor and building materials; cash to be paid in advance."

C: "Fifty percent, sir? That's too much for most families."

S: "That's as may be, but if you don't contribute 50 percent, your long-term ownership-feeling won't be strong enough; 49 percent is not enough."

C: "Okay, you'll get your 50 percent. Will we then get our dam?"

S: "That depends on so many factors: Can we finance the other 50 percent? Is it technically feasible? Do we have enough time? Anyway, always remember that for you the learning process is more important than the result. See you in the next meeting."[2]

Bremer confirms that while this dialog might sound like a caricature, the situation it portrays really happened. As a result, not a single dam or retention basin was built, but the target group was taught, in theory, how to help themselves. The concept of helping people to help themselves is often explained with the saying "Don't give fish to the poor, teach them how to fish." Bremer doesn't think much of such pearls of wisdom, even when they sound plausible at first glance: "All over the world, people who live by the water know how to fish, whether with rods, nets, fish traps, or spears, and how to preserve fish by smoking it, drying it, or soaking it in brine."[3] Nobody needs development workers for that.

Of course, the fishing analogy is not meant to be taken literally but to serve as an example. Nevertheless, Bremer criticizes the very principle of development aid, which is based on so-called "projects." Although there is so much talk about sustainability today, these projects are rarely sustainable. Hardly anyone is concerned with what has become of such projects, for example, ten years after they have come to an end. If you drive through the African countryside, you will constantly pass rusting project signs, sometimes even from several donors in the same place: they look like grave markers, the last remaining indication that something was there at one time. There is no money left, not even enough to dismantle the signs at the end of the project; at best they are used by village blacksmiths to make cooking pots.

While they were running, many of these projects were quite successful, as there was enough money for materials, operating resources, vehicles, and high salaries. But once the funding dried up, it became clear that these highly subsidized projects were all nothing more than "uneconomic flashes in the pan," of which nothing remained once they ended.[4]

Bremer is most familiar with Côte d'Ivoire (Ivory Coast), a country in West Africa and the world's largest exporter of cocoa. As early as 1977, Bremer, an ethnologist, sociologist, and development economist, wrote his doctoral thesis on the history of cocoa production in Côte d'Ivoire. He still lives there to this day. His assessment of the development aid projects in the country is harsh: with the exception of a forestry project, not one of the twenty-four completed projects has had a long-term impact. "Assessed against this criterion," he concluded, "they were all failures or just flashes in the pan, costing a total of €125 million."[5]

Another of Bremer's examples concerns the construction and maintenance of a veterinary pharmacy in Burundi's economic capital, Bujumbura. The project lasted twenty-two years with the same seconded specialist throughout, but became financially unviable shortly after funding ended. It had to close. "This is what happens," says Bremer, "when development aid enters private-sector terrain, but dispenses with needs analyses, business plans, and profitability calculations, and thus uses taxpayers' money to set up a subsidized playground for seconded professionals."[6]

When the funding runs out, a project is terminated, although this doesn't prevent the development workers from setting up a similar project a few years later in the same or another country, the failure of which is equally certain from the outset.

Bremer's overall conclusion is therefore devastating: "This has been going on for fifty years, and the entire international development aid industry, which is financed with public funds, lives from this kind of project. The alleged beneficiaries, the poor farmers, who are supposed to be helped by these projects, are no less poor at the end and are once again left to fend for themselves. Instead of helping the poor, these projects create countless jobs for seconded professionals and their supervisors at the aid organizations' headquarters."[7]

William Easterly, Professor of Economics and African Studies at New York University, describes development aid as largely useless, often even counterproductive. Here is just one example from his book *The White Man's Burden: Why the West's Efforts to Aid the Rest Have Done So Much Ill and So Little Good*. Over the course of two decades, $2 billion in development aid was spent on road construction in Tanzania. But the road network did not improve in the slightest. Because the roads were not maintained, they deteriorated faster than the donors could build new ones, Easterly reports. The "growth industry" in Tanzania, on the other hand, was a gigantic bureaucracy. "Tanzania produced more than 2,400 reports a year for its aid donors, who sent the beleaguered recipient 1,000 missions of donor officials per year." Foreign aid, Easterly notes, did not supply what the poor needed (roads), it supplied a lot of what the poor had little use for (bureaucracy).[8]

Born in Zambia, Dambisa Moyo has lived in the United States since the early 1990s, where she continued her education with a scholarship. She first studied chemistry at the American University in Washington, DC, and, after receiving her Bachelor's degree, completed an MBA program in finance. She also completed a Master's degree at Harvard University's Kennedy School of Government and received a DPhil in economics from Oxford University. In her book *Dead Aid*, she takes issue with development aid: A World Bank study shows that more than 85 percent of aid money ends up being used for purposes other than originally intended, often diverted to unproductive projects.[9] Even where the money is used for projects that actually make sense in themselves, any short-term positive impacts are often counteracted by negative long-term consequences, for example because aid projects destroy local companies in the countries they are supposed to be helping.

In many cases, fads dictate which topics receive the most funds. For example, a hype developed around eco-farms. According to Bremer, "for twelve years they remained an inconsequential playground for seconded experts and their technical experts, who pursued the ecological and/or site-appropriate agriculture that has become so fashionable. All in all, about €20 million has been sunk into the Savannah sand on these projects."[10]

The general public in the donor countries is not interested. The projects are so far away and whether they really make a difference or not is a subject to be debated between academics, if at all. Politicians and the media are understandably more concerned with the issues that preoccupy and interest voters and readers in the donor countries, and not with the question of whether the billions in development aid are being used wisely. At most, politicians or the media sometimes critically enquire whether it makes sense, for example, for Germany to send large payments of development aid to China—€630 million in 2017 alone.[11]

Proponents of development aid like to point out that global poverty has declined massively in recent decades: in 1981, the absolute poverty rate was 42.7 percent; by 2000, it had fallen to 27.8 percent; and in 2023 it was less than nine percent.[12] That is an incredible success, but it came not because of, but in spite of, development aid. Above all, the decline in the number of poor people worldwide was due to the development of two populous states in Asia—China and, to a lesser extent, India. I have written extensively about China in my books *The Power of Capitalism* and *In Defense of Capitalism*. I would therefore like to repeat only this much at this point: at the end of the 1950s, during the greatest socialist experiment in human history, Mao's Great Leap Forward, about forty-five million Chinese died, most of them from hunger. And even in 1981, after the end of Mao's socialist planned economy, 88 percent of Chinese people were living in extreme poverty. It is only through the introduction of private property and capitalist reforms that the number of Chinese living in extreme poverty has fallen to about 0.5 percent today.

Vietnam, which was still one of the poorest countries in the world in the early 1990s, has also reduced the proportion of its population that live in poverty from 80 percent to less than 5 percent as a result of the *Doi Moi* free-market reforms that began in 1986; I have more to say on this in Chapter Three.

But let's return to the topic at hand: development aid. Is the picture painted by authors such as Frank Bremer, William Easterly, and Dambisa Moyo too one-sided? In 2000, a study by the American economists Craig Burnside and David Dollar[13] on "Aid, Policies, and Growth" garnered a great deal of attention. They tried to prove that under certain conditions—especially where recipient countries were well governed—development aid contributed to growth.

The economist Tomi Ovaska reviewed the results in a paper published in 2003 ("The Failure of Development Aid") which presented calculations for eighty-six developing countries between 1975 and 1998. He came to the conclusion that development aid actually had a negative effect on growth. "In particular, it was found, that a 1 percent increase in aid as a percent of GDP decreased annual real GDP per capita growth by 3.65 percent." Nor could Ovaska find any confirmation in the data for Burnside and Dollar's thesis that better quality of government leads to greater aid effectiveness.[14] He therefore arrived at a different recommendation: "Helping and encouraging developing countries to create business environments that are compatible with free markets is a promising and a potentially cost-effective way to unleash the individual effort and creativity in those countries."[15]

William Easterly, whom I have already cited above, used the same data as Burnside and Dollar in a paper also published in 2003 ("Can Foreign Aid Buy Growth?"), combined it with additional data, and concluded that claims that development aid has a positive effect in countries with good political framework conditions does not stand up to closer scrutiny either.[16] A detailed statistical study covering a period of twenty-four years—from 1970 to 1993—revealed that development aid has done nothing for the economic growth of recipient countries.[17]

Easterly also points out that "the World Bank reviews only 5 percent of its loans after three to ten years following the last disbursement for development impact."[18] Ultimately, this means that people are not interested in the impacts of development aid—or they deliberately do not look more closely at the results.

Four years later, Easterly published another paper on the subject: "Was Development Assistance a Mistake?" Over the past forty-two years, $568 billion (in 2007 dollars) had flowed to Africa, but no measurable growth in real GDP per capita had been recorded. The top quarter of all aid recipient countries have received 17 percent of GDP in aid over these forty-two years, but per capita GDP growth has been close to zero.[19] At the same time, the countries that have experienced high growth, especially India, China, and Vietnam, have received comparatively little development aid.[20]

Easterly's overall assessment of development aid is scathing: "an emphasis on loans made rather than on the results of those loans, a surplus of reports that no one reads, a fondness for grand frameworks and world summits, moral exhortations to everyone rather than any agency taking responsibility for any one thing, foreign technical experts to whom no one is listening, health clinics without medicines, schools without textbooks, roads and water systems built but not maintained, aid-financed governments that stay in power despite corruption and economic mismanagement, and so on."[21]

What really helps are not experts with the presumption of knowledge, but spontaneous developments of the market, developments that have to come from below.[22] The free-market economy, Easterly explains in his book *White Man's Burden*, works, but it cannot be imposed from above.[23]

By its nature—and in distinct contrast to socialist models of economic planning—capitalism is a social order that emerges as the result of a spontaneous development, rather than a system that relies on human invention and design. The consequence of this realization for Easterly is greater humility: "So the West cannot design a comprehensive reform for a poor country that creates benevolent laws and good institutions to make markets work. We have seen that the rules that make markets work reflect a complex bottom-up search for social norms, networks of relationships, and formal laws and institutions that have the most payoff. To make things worse, these norms, networks, and institutions change in response to changed circumstances and their own past history."[24]

To demonstrate this, Easterly presents an example from China: In the small village of Xiaogang in Anhui province (the heart of China's rice-growing region) about twenty families held a secret meeting in 1978. The villagers were desperate because the collectivization of agriculture and the abolition of private property had led to hunger and extreme poverty, as it had in the Soviet Union before. In many villages in China, people therefore *de facto* reintroduced private property, although this was actually forbidden. They divided up the land and everyone was allowed to keep what they produced on their piece of land.

Although the villagers kept their arrangement secret, rice production in Xiaogang shot up and the results were too spectacular to stay secret for long. When the residents of other villages found out what was going on in Xiaogang, they also put individual farming into place.[25] By this time, Deng Xiaoping had started his free-market reforms in China, and the state no longer stopped people from looking for better, free-market solutions.

But long before the official ban on private farming was lifted in 1982, there were spontaneous initiatives by peasants all over China who, contrary to the socialist creed, effectively reintroduced private ownership.[26] The results were incredibly positive: agricultural production increased rapidly, and people were no longer left to starve. By 1983, almost all agriculture in China had been de-collectivized. Mao's great socialist experiment, to which so many millions of people had fallen victim, was over. In this book, I use the examples of Vietnam and Poland to show that governments play an important role, but that the reforms they "impose" from the top down sometimes only sanction what was already happening from the bottom up.

In 2009, the Danish economist Martin Paldam from the University of Aarhus published an article in the renowned *Journal of Economic Surveys* entitled "The Aid Effectiveness Literature: The Sad Results of Forty Years of Research." Paldam had scrutinized ninety-seven scientific studies on the effectiveness of development aid. He conducted several meta-analyses, i.e., statistical procedures that summarize and evaluate the results of numerous studies on the same issue. His findings: "Our three meta-analyses of the Aid-Effectiveness-Literature have failed to find evidence of a significantly positive effect of aid. Consequently, if there is an effect, it must be small. Development aid is an activity that has proved difficult to do right."[27]

In June 2017, the German economists Axel Dreher and Sarah Langlotz took another look at the same questions and examined the effects of development aid on ninety-six recipient countries in the period from 1974 to 2009. They found that bilateral aid can do nothing to increase economic growth. In the years of the Cold War, according to another finding, development aid actually had a negative impact on economic growth. "We also investigate the effect of aid on savings, consumption, and investment, and do not find any effect of aid in the overall sample or our sub-samples."[28]

The authors almost apologize for publishing these depressing findings, but feel obliged to do so, as many publications are characterized by a well-meaning narrow-mindedness toward the topic: "We still believe that it is important to show, and publish, these results, as the published literature on the effectiveness of aid tends to be over-optimistic, due to institutional biases of the authors in the aid effectiveness literature and the well-known bias of journals to publish (only) significant results."[29]

As we have seen, it does not seem that development aid helps to fight poverty in the long term. However, this does not mean that we should stop providing humanitarian aid, for example in response to natural disasters or famine. Such aid is right and important. But that is not what is meant by development aid or development cooperation.

If development aid does not help with economic growth, then perhaps it helps with the development of democratic structures in a society? This is not the case either, as a study published in April 2005 shows. The authors, Simeon Djankov, Jose G. Montalvo, and Marta Reynal-Querol, examined data from 108 recipient countries spanning a period of almost forty years, and concluded that "foreign aid has a negative impact on democracy."[30] If the findings of so many scientific studies are so clear-cut, why does the belief that development aid is the best way to lift nations out of poverty so doggedly persist? I think it is because of what I call zero-sum beliefs. Many people believe that poor countries are only poor because rich countries have taken something away from them. The implication is that the rich countries have to give up some of their wealth and then the poor countries will be better off.

But this is an illusion because the zero-sum assumptions on which this belief is based are false. In economic sociology, a zero-sum game describes a constellation in which the sum of the payouts to the players is zero. One player's gain is automatically another player's loss. Non-zero-sum games, on the other hand, are games in which the sum of the payouts to the players is not constant. In such games, both parties can win or lose, or one party can win without the other losing, and so on.

Researchers believe that the zero-sum belief has its roots in pre-capitalist societies where situations with limited resources were the norm. In his 2010 paper "Zero-Sum Bias: Perceived Competition Despite Unlimited Resources," Daniel V. Meegan concludes that, "When resources are limited, the allocation of desirable resources means that those resources will soon be depleted."[31]

The American economist Paul H. Rubin has shown that folk economics, or popular or amateur ideas of economic life, are entirely focused on the question of the distribution of wealth, not on how that wealth is produced.[32] "The key point is this: folk economics is the economics of wealth allocation, not production. Naive people, or those untrained in economics, think of prices as allocating wealth but not as influencing allocation of resources or production of goods and services. In folk economics, the amount of a good traded—whether in aggregate or by each individual— is fixed and independent of price. Moreover, each individual is concerned with the distribution of wealth and income, not with any efficiency gains from economic activity."[33]

Rubin attributes this kind of thinking to conditioning in the human brain, which he explains in terms of evolutionary biology.[34] Over millions of years, there were hardly any improvements in technology or growth. The pace of change in primitive societies was so slow that individuals could hardly perceive it during the course of their lives. Everyone lived in a world with seemingly unchanging technology, and no advantage existed for people who had an understanding of growth—precisely because there was virtually none. There was also hardly any division of labor, apart from the division of labor between children and adults and between men and women. Trade was not an expression of a systematic division of labor, but rather the result of chance—merely by luck, or perhaps by geography, someone had something in abundance that another could use. If people in such societies had advantages or disadvantages, then those stemmed mostly from one person's not treating another fairly, or by his holding a real but serendipitous advantage over the other. Therefore, according to Rubin, people developed a strong sense to recognize and avoid situations in which they could be victimized or cheated by others.

In pre-capitalist societies, the wealth of some was indeed often based on robbery and the exercise of power, i.e., the losses of others. However, the market system is not based on robbery and is not a zero-sum game. It is based on getting rich by satisfying the needs of as many consumers as possible. That is the logic of the market. And the economic growth characteristic of capitalist systems makes it possible for some people and also whole nations to become richer, without this necessarily happening at the expense of other people or nations, who would automatically become poorer, so to speak. I would like to show this here by taking the examples of two countries that were both mired in extreme poverty thirty years ago—Vietnam and Poland.

CHAPTER THREE

VIETNAM: *DOI MOI*—RISE OF THE DRAGON

Eight-year-old Phung Xuan Vu and his ten-year-old brother were responsible for fetching food for their family, which was in the constant grip of hunger. And this, before the free-market *Doi Moi* reforms began to take effect in Vietnam, was only possible with ration cards. One of the family's most important possessions was a booklet of vouchers for food. As the elder of the two children, Vu's brother took care of the booklet, knowing that if he lost it, the family would have nothing to eat. The vouchers inside were printed on waxy yellow tissue paper. They meant the difference between going hungry and having something to eat, although it was never enough. The vouchers had to be redeemed at food distribution centers. People often had to wait hours, sometimes all day, to get a little food, and those who wanted a better chance of leaving with food came at night. As Nancy K. Napier and Dau Thuy Ha relate in their book *The Bridge Generation Việt Nam: Spanning Wartime to Boomtime*, for which they conducted interviews with a wide variety of Vietnamese people, including Vu: "The children, along with their neighbors, waited for hours. Some people arrived at 2 a.m., or 4 a.m., or 5 a.m. when it was still dark. Some left a basket or brick to hold their spot in line and went off to another activity. If the sun was up, school children studied and did their homework while waiting. They stood in the rain, when the ground became muddy and slippery. They stood in the heat, when they nearly fainted from thirst and weakness."[1]

They were already queuing up before the food was even delivered, in the hope that it would arrive at some point. Families sent their children, others sent people ahead to stand in line for them—and of course you had to wait your turn. Once it was finally your turn, you often found yourself face-to-face with harsh officials. As Vu explained to Napier and Ha: "The officials were not friendly. They were bossy and had power. We felt like we had to beg for the food that was rightfully ours."[2]

The families had no choice, said Vu, but to accept whatever it was the officials threw into their bags: "We held our sacks open for the officials to dump rice into. The workers took a bucket, scooped rice from a big sack on the cart and put it onto a scale to be sure they didn't give us more than our family's limit. We knew the officials sometimes put rocks in the sacks with the rice, so we got less rice than we were entitled to, and often the rice was old or moldy. We also knew that the workers kept the good rice, if there was any, for themselves or their friends or they sold it on the black market to make money. That made us angry but we could not fight or argue with the officials. What could we do, as children?"[3]

The amount of food you got depended on your family's status. State employees received more, factory workers less. If there was not enough rice, people were given wheat instead, even though hardly anyone knew what to do with it. But even if they knew how to bake bread, it was difficult because they couldn't normally get hold of the other ingredients they needed. In any case, they needed electricity to heat the oven, but electricity was only available for a few hours a day. And the family did not use the electricity for the oven, but to turn on a lamp or listen to an old radio. Sometimes the electricity suddenly cut out, and they had to light a candle. Some families stole electricity, but that was dangerous.[4]

Vu's family was very proud to own an old bicycle. Although it was fairly ancient, to them it was like owning a Rolls Royce. At that time, in the 1980s and early 1990s, almost all Vietnamese people rode bicycles. Today in Hanoi, you hardly see any bicycles—about 85 percent of the vehicles on the streets are motorbikes and mopeds.

The American Nancy K. Napier compiled first-hand accounts from Vietnamese people together with Dau Thuy Ha. They divided their book between the time before and after the *Doi Moi* reforms, and headed the chapter on the time before with the word "Hunger." She taught at the National Economics University in Hanoi from 1994. She remembers what her colleagues would say to her when she gained some weight: "Nancy, you are fat!" She taught her Vietnamese co-workers that you should never, under any circumstances, tell an American woman she was fat. They did not understand: "Oh, but that means you are prosperous. You have enough food to eat so you can be fat. You must be happy!"[5]

When I gave a lecture at the same university in 2022, I saw well-dressed professors and young, budding academics who were full of ambition to make something of their lives. Nancy K. Napier also recalls wondering why there were so few birds in Hanoi. When she asked her colleagues, they looked at her in bewilderment, as if she were not quite right in the head. They explained to her that people who were hungry caught birds to eat, even sparrows.[6] Many people were malnourished or suffering from vitamin A deficiency. "Young mothers sometimes could not produce enough milk for their children, so some of them boiled rice and fed the 'rice milk' to their babies, hoping that the nutrients would suffice."[7]

Bach Ngoc Chien remembers: "When I was a teenager, I was always hungry. My family of five divided three bowls of rice for lunch and three bowls for dinner. We children shared one bowl for breakfast. We almost never had meat, except on two occasions: Lunar New Year and my grandfather's death anniversary. In 1988, in my last year of high school, I think I weighed less than eighty-eight pounds."[8]

Even Soviet Belarus seemed like a paradise in comparison. Luong Ngoc Khanh, who today owns a number of large companies, was sent to Minsk in 1983 to learn Russian: "At the time, Russia [he means Belarus] was like paradise. We had apples to eat, milk to drink, meat to eat. In Vietnam, there was a shortage of all of those things."[9]

Today, the Vietnamese call this period "*Thoi Bao Cap*" ("subsidy period"). It was the time of the socialist planned economy before Vietnam successively became a market economy as a result of the *Doi Moi* reforms. Vietnam has changed massively as a result of these reforms, and that is the theme of this chapter. In her book *Vietnam und sein Transformationsweg* (in English, *Vietnam and Its Transformative Journey*), which reflects on developments in Vietnam since 1986, Tam T.T. Nguyen is clear: "Poverty in Vietnam has gone from being a majority problem to a minority problem."[10]

In 1990, with a per capita GDP of $98, Vietnam was the poorest country in the world, behind Somalia ($130) and Sierra Leone ($163).[11] How backward and poor Vietnam was, even in comparison with other socialist countries, can be seen from the following figures: electricity produced per inhabitant in 1985 was 4,656 kwh in Hungary, 6,839 kWh in the GDR (East Germany), 3,702 kWh in Poland and 87 kWh in Vietnam. In 1960, average incomes were 669.80 rubles in Hungary and 581.80 in Poland. Twenty-four years later (in 1984!), the average income in Vietnam was equivalent to a paltry fifty rubles.[12]

Before the economic reforms began, every bad harvest led to hunger, and Vietnam relied on support from the UN's World Food Programme and financial assistance from the Soviet Union and other Eastern Bloc countries.[13] As late as 1993, 79.7 percent of the Vietnamese population were living in poverty. By 2006, the rate had fallen to 50.6 percent. In 2020, it was only 5 percent.[14]

Vietnam is now one of the most dynamic countries in the world, with a vibrant economy that creates great opportunities for hardworking people and entrepreneurs. From a country that, before the market reforms began, was unable to produce enough rice to feed its own population, it has become one of the world's largest rice exporters, as well as a major electronics exporter.

However, whenever I talk to people about Vietnam, I notice that they usually know very little about the country. Many are surprised when I tell them that Vietnam has more inhabitants than any European country. With almost 100 million inhabitants, Vietnam has a bigger population than Germany, Turkey, the UK, France, Italy or Spain; it is almost twice as large as South Korea and sixteen times that of Singapore.

A Country at War

When many people think of Vietnam, the first thing that comes to mind is the Vietnam War, by which they mean the war waged by the US in this Southeast Asian country from 1955 to 1975. What they do not know is that this was only one stage of the longer Indochina War, which began in 1946 and lasted almost thirty years. And this was not the only war that ravaged Vietnam. Rarely in human history has a single country been the target of so many conquests by its neighbors. Over the last 1,000 years, the periods of war have been longer than those of peace, and Vietnam has had to defend itself repeatedly against foreign invaders and occupiers: the Chinese and the Mongols, the Japanese, and the French.

In the mid-nineteenth century, the country came under French colonial rule. During the Second World War, it was occupied by the Japanese, and in 1945 it returned to French rule until the French were defeated on May 7, 1954 in the Battle of Điện Biên Phủ. The country was then divided into the northern Democratic Republic of Vietnam, with Hanoi as its capital, and the southern Republic of Vietnam, with Saigon as its capital. This was followed by the war most people know as the Vietnam War, in which the communist North and the National Liberation Front of South Vietnam (supported by the Soviet Union and China) fought against the US-backed South Vietnam.

North Vietnam was led by HôChí Minh, who is still revered in Vietnam today. On January 27, 1973, US Secretary of State Henry Kissinger and HôChí Minh's successor Lê Đức Thọ agreed to a cessation of hostilities. The war then continued without direct US involvement (although the US continued to supply weapons to South Vietnam). It ended with the capture of Saigon on April 30, 1975, which was followed by the unconditional surrender of South Vietnam on May 1, 1975. Then, on July 2, 1975, North and South Vietnam were reunited under the name Socialist Republic of Vietnam. Hanoi has been the capital ever since and Saigon is officially called HôChí Minh City, although many Vietnamese still call it Saigon.

The war devastated the country. Some 14–15 million tons of bombs and explosives fell on Vietnam—ten times as many as had been dropped on Germany in the Second World War.[15] The chemical weapons of mass destruction used by the US, including the defoliant Agent Orange, not only struck the communist liberation army, they also hit the civilian population. Napalm bombs also inflicted heavy casualties among the civilian population. The South Vietnamese alone lost 1.5 million people, including 300,000 civilians.[16] By the end of the war, there were almost one million orphans in South Vietnam, several hundred thousand people had been driven into drug addiction and prostitution, and there were at least one million war invalids, often with severe physical disabilities. Huge numbers of people were traumatized.[17] The US military suffered 58,200 casualties, plus another 300,000 wounded.

Civilian losses in North Vietnam were lower than in the South, but it lost far more soldiers.[18] In *Vietnam und sein Trans-formationsweg,* Tam T.T. Nguyen provides an objective appraisal: "In the North, the war destroyed the main industrial centers and basic infrastructure [...]. All industrial enterprises were destroyed. As were three of the six largest cities, twelve out of twenty-nine provincial capitals, and two-thirds of all villages. All electricity plants, railway stations, ports, bridges, roads and the entire railway network were also totally destroyed."[19] Nguyen also assesses the extent of the losses in the South, where two-thirds of villages were also devastated, large swathes of forest were obliterated and twenty million farmers lost their homes

With their victory over the Americans, this already proud country became even prouder, for they had defeated the greatest military superpower in history. But their pride suffered over the next ten years as the introduction of a socialist planned economy had a devastating effect on the entire country. Vietnam was the poorest country in the region. While Asian countries that took the capitalist path—for example, South Korea, Hong Kong, and Singapore—achieved incredible growth and escaped poverty, most people in Vietnam lived in bitter poverty, even ten years after the war had come to an end.

According to Napier and Dau Thuy Ha, "After the fall of Saigon, the Vietnamese from the north expected all would be fine. They dreamed of a better life, after decades of occupation and fighting—with invasions from the Japanese, the French, and the Americans."[20] In his 1969 testament, President HôChí Minh had promised: "The American invaders defeated, we will rebuild our land ten times more beautiful."[21]

Socialist Planned Economy in the North and the South

Once the French had been defeated, HôChí Minh established a system modelled on the Soviet socialist planned economy in the North of Vietnam. The communists wanted to transfer this same system to South Vietnam following their victory over the US. Briefly, there was even talk of implementing a "one country, two systems" approach, with a free-market economy in the South and a socialist, planned economy in the North, but the idea was quickly abandoned.[22]

In August 1975, the Twenty-Fourth Session of the Central Committee of the Party of the Working People of Vietnam (PdWV, as the Communist Party of Vietnam was then known) decided that the North should continue making progress on the path toward socialism, and that socialism should also be introduced in the South.[23] In December 1976, at its Fourth Congress, the communist party, now known as the Communist Party of Vietnam (CPV) , adopted its first Five-Year Plan for reunified Vietnam, with the aim of also transforming the South in line with socialist ideology.

During 1977 and 1978, the collectivization of agriculture and the nationalization of almost 30,000 privately-owned small businesses began in HôChí Minh City. The party justified its policies by pointing to the fact that until then the state controlled "only" about 50 percent of wholesale trade and 40 percent of small-scale trade in South Vietnam.[24] Most companies were in the hands of Chinese, so there were few scruples about taking radical action.

When it came to collectivization, the communists in the South were a bit more cautious. Many peasants in the South regarded collectivization as particularly unjust because the communists had previously given them land to secure their support and now wanted to take it away from them again. "NLF [National Liberation Front] members, among others, had won rural support partly because they helped push the redistribution of farmland among tenant farmers and landholders who held small portions of land. The complete elimination of private landownership would have been a severe affront to this recent working relationship between the Party and the farmers."[25]

When collectivization began in the South, many peasants resisted, some left their land or sold their animals or farming implements because they did not want to work in collectives.[26] In 1980, only 24.5 percent of the rural population in the South worked in collectives, compared to 97 percent in the North.[27]

Collectivization and nationalization triggered a severe crisis that lasted until the early 1980s.[28] It soon became clear that there was no hope of achieving the ambitious goals of the Five-Year Plan adopted at the Fourth Party Congress.

The communists reacted the same way that most politicians who miss their targets do: instead of admitting that they were on the wrong track (this realization followed only a few years later), they became convinced that their policies of abolishing private property and socialist transformation had to be accelerated. This had a particularly disastrous effect in the agricultural sector, as Claudia Pfeifer explains in her book *Konfuzius und Marx am Roten Fluss. Vietnamesische Reformkonzepte nach 1975* (in English, *Confucius and Marx on the Red River. Vietnamese reforms after 1975*): "The peasants in South Vietnam reacted by restricting production, which was primarily oriented towards their own needs [...]. Within a few months, the agricultural sector almost completely collapsed. In 1978, only 190 kg of rice or 238 kg of food were available per capita, compared to 240/274 kg in 1976."[29]

The communists should have known what would happen. After all, similar policies for collectivizing agriculture had already failed in China and the Soviet Union. In a paper for the World Institute for Development Economic Research, Finn Tarp reports that: "In any case, individual land ownership was abolished in 1980 in the whole country in line with the politics of the socialist transformation that had been promoted in North Vietnam after the adoption of the 1959 Constitution. This course of action was taken even if the collectivized production sector was clearly inefficient."[30]

According to Claudia Pfeifer, when it came to investment, the government favored state-owned cooperatives: they received 40 percent of all state funds, despite contributing only 5 percent of total agricultural production.[31] The planned economy simply did not work: less than 10 percent of the cultivated area for annual crops could be artificially irrigated and drained, even though pumps were available for about 40 percent of the area—power shortages and blackouts often made their use impossible. Only 30 percent of the agriculture sector's electricity demands were satisfied.[32]

Members of the state collectives were awarded points and these points were in turn used to calculate their pay. "The shortcoming was that work points were based on the duration of the job and not the quality or even the quantity of the work performed. This encouraged members to slack off, be sloppy, or to arrive late at their jobs."[33]

Bach Ngoc Chien recalls that his mother worked for a cooperative, in a system that did not reward members for the amount of rice they produced, but only counted how many days they had worked. If his mother worked thirty days, she got thirty points, which gave her the right to a defined share of the harvest. If she had worked only twenty days, she got twenty points and correspondingly less.[34]

In 1980, Vietnam produced only fourteen million tons of rice, despite the fact that the country needed sixteen million tons to meet its own population's basic needs. During the period of the second Five-Year Plan (1976 to 1980), Vietnam was forced to import eight to nine million tons of rice and other foodstuffs.[35] Every failed harvest led to immediate food shortages. "Food-rationing was reintroduced, and Vietnam had to rely on large amounts of food aid support from the World Food Programme and on financial and material support from the former Soviet Union and the Eastern European countries."[36]

If you compare the objectives set out in the Five-Year Plan of 1976 with what actually happened, the extent of the failure becomes clear: the Five-Year Plan envisaged an increase in gross domestic product of 13–14 percent per year for 1976 to 1980; in fact, it was only 0.4 percent—and this with a rapidly growing population. According to the plan, agricultural production was to increase by 8–10 percent per year; in fact, it went up by 1.9 percent. And for industrial production, the plan envisaged annual increases of 16–18 percent; in reality, Vietnam achieved an annual average of just 0.6 percent.[37]

In the entire northern half of the country, the per capita supply of paddy rice declined by about one-third in the second half of the 1970s alone. By year, this decline was as follows: in 1976, the per capita supply was 15.4 kilograms per month, dropping to 12 kg in 1977, 11.6 kg in 1978, 11.9 kg in 1979, and 10.4 kg in 1980.

The idea of agricultural collectives had already failed before in North Vietnam and was now failing in South Vietnam as well. And the results of the collectives were worse the larger they were.[38] A 1979 study of collectives in the Red River Delta found that collectives that farmed between 301 and 400 hectares had a net surplus of 408 đ`ông per hectare, while those farming more than 500 hectares had a net yield of only seventy-three đ`ông per hectare.[39]

The failure of collectivization was also evident from the fact that most of the yield was produced on a fraction of the land, namely the portion that was privately farmed. From 1976 to 1988, more than 60 percent of the total income of cooperative members came from the 5 percent of land they were allowed to keep after 95 percent of the land had been collectivized.[40]

Interestingly, this ratio was quite similar in the Soviet Union: although private farmland in the USSR accounted for less than 5 percent of total farmland, it supplied more than 70 percent of potatoes, about 70 percent of milk, and close to 90 percent of eggs until well into the 1950s.[41]

Besides the failed economic policy, sanctions against Vietnam exacerbated the country's economic crisis. The sanctions had been imposed in response to Vietnam's war with Cambodia in January 1979. If anything, Vietnam should be thanked for helping the opponents of one of the most brutal terror regimes in history, the Pol Pot regime in Cambodia.[42] But China supported Pol Pot as an ally against Soviet influence in Southeast Asia and not only stopped supporting Vietnam politically and economically, but actually went to war against its comparatively small neighbor in February and March 1979. This was ostensibly over border disputes but, in reality, Beijing turned on Hanoi because it was worried about Moscow gaining a stronger influence in the region.

Let's get back to the economy: at first, South Vietnam's new rulers declared that they only wanted to nationalize foreign-owned enterprises. Vietnamese-owned enterprises were transformed into so-called parastatals (enterprises with state participation). However, this was meant to be only a temporary measure, as the plan was that gradually all enterprises would become fully state-owned.[43]

In early 1978, Finn Tarp explains, 1,500 private enterprises in the South of Vietnam were transformed into 650 state-owned enterprises: "But in spite of the fact that none of the industry targets set for the 1976 to 1980 Five-Year Plan were met, state ownership was pushed forward, and in 1986, SOEs accounted for 40 per cent of GDP."[44]

The same problems arose in industry as in agriculture. Production stagnated, and state-owned industrial production actually declined by 10 percent from 1976 to 1980.[45] Nevertheless, the Sixth Consultation of the CPV Central Committee in 1979 marked the beginning of a slow relaxation of radical socialist policies. Now, Vietnam was experiencing what had been seen time and again since Lenin's New Economic Policy in the Soviet Union of the 1920s. The communists realized that their ideology had brought the country to the brink of an existential crisis and were forced to make free-market concessions. A dualism of state and private forms of ownership developed at all economic levels. Claudia Pfeifer offers the following assessment: "At the beginning of the 1980s, the free market, in which prices were based on cost calculations and supply and demand, was once again allowed. At the same time, the first cuts to subsidies for state-owned enterprises were introduced."[46]

To some extent, these initial reforms only legitimized what had already taken place as spontaneous developments in several villages. Many agricultural collectives and even state-owned enterprises had long been turning a blind eye to official state rules and regulations. They refused to work in collectives and concluded unauthorized contracts (*"khoan chui"*) between collectives and families or between state farms and private traders. This practice was called *"pha rao,"* or fence breaking.[47]

Some authors even go so far as to see the real source of the reforms in these spontaneous grassroots developments in the countryside rather than in the party, which only sanctioned them. "It is closer to the truth of the matter," explains Vu Le Thao Chi, "that the state served more as an agent of adjustments and, in this, sanctioned the manner of the ordinary farmers' efforts to survive the unpredictably winding path."[48]

There were already changes in the countryside before the official launch of the major reforms in the 1980s. The farmers concentrated their work on the little land they owned themselves, i.e., approximately 5 percent of total farmland, because they could sell the goods they produced here at market prices. Tran Thi Anh-Dao and other scholars stress that the reform process in Vietnam began "with evidence-based practices at the microeconomic (local) level that were then applied at the macroeconomic (national) level."[49]

The provinces in the Mekong Delta, for example, abolished the rationing subsidy system (*bao cấp*) as early as the 1980s and opted for a market-based system. According to Tran Thi Anh-Dao, "Without such illegal or pilot procedures, there is evidence that market mechanisms could never have emerged so rapidly."[50] Some reforms merely legalized the continuation of private sector structures in the South after the end of the war.

Here we see parallels with developments in China. There, too, movements from below, for example those initiated by peasants, were at least as important as top-down, state-initiated reforms. After the bitter experience of the Great Leap Forward, the largest socialist experiment in history under Mao Zedong, in which forty-five million Chinese citizens died, a growing number of rural peasants seized the initiative and decided to reintroduce private ownership of farmland, even though this was officially prohibited. But it quickly became apparent that the yields from private farming were much higher, and so party officials in China also let the people have their way.

The first experiments were carried out in particularly poor "beggar villages," where officials concluded that if things go wrong here, it's not so bad, because you can't fall when you're already at rock bottom. In one of these small villages, the party leadership allowed the farmers to cultivate the particularly low-yield fields as private farmers. Soon after they were allowed to do so, the land yielded three times as much as it had while it had been operated as a collective.

Long before the ban on private farming was officially lifted in 1982, there were spontaneous initiatives by farmers all over China to reintroduce private ownership, contrary to the socialist creed. The result was extremely positive: People were no longer forced to go hungry and agricultural yields increased significantly. So, we see from the examples of China and Vietnam that capitalism, unlike socialism, cannot be decreed by state orders; it grows in a spontaneous process from below, and the best thing political leaders can do is not to disrupt or prevent this process.

The initial focus of reforms in Vietnam was on agriculture, which was by far the most important economic sector at the time. The state loosened its tight grip on agriculture, for example, with the introduction in 1981 of what was known as "Directive 100": "Cooperative land was distributed to farming families for short-term use and farmers were responsible for planting, harvesting, and manuring [...]. Directive 100 made a breakthrough and was a historic turn-around in agricultural policy, which created new incentives for farmers to raise agricultural outputs during the period 1982–85."[51]

Vu Le Thao Chi has the following to say about this directive: "It placed the unwritten custom of family-based production into an officially sanctioned framework."[52]

In the early 1980s, a number of reforms were introduced in Vietnam, as they had been in other socialist countries in Eastern Europe. Firms would now be responsible for their own profits and losses. Enterprises could decide for themselves what to do with any excess profits. One major caveat, writes Tam T.T. Nguyen, was that "Production volumes and values, production profits, transfers to the state, wage bills, state investment funds, materials, equipment, goods to be supplied, as well as the prices of most products were still predetermined. Some free markets for agricultural products were allowed, but on a very limited scale. And what was produced was still distributed by the state."[53]

It was the first modest reforms that often only legalized what had already been taking place spontaneously in the countryside as well as in the cities. David Wurfel finds that, "For instance, when materials were short, goods could be sold in the open market to raise cash to buy supplies, or perhaps to pay bonuses to workers and thus raise productivity. Though largely illegal, these initiatives became more and more widespread. Thus, the first key reform decree for state industry in January 1981 required factories to register all activities they conducted outside the plan at the same time that it allowed them to acquire and dispose of resources as needed to increase their supply of inputs."[54]

Although the situation improved somewhat as a result of the reforms, supplies of basic foods could still not meet people's needs, and Vietnam remained one of the five poorest countries in the world.[55]

Officially, there were about four million unemployed people in Vietnam, but in April 1987 the Vietnamese ambassador told the foreign minister of Hungary in a confidential conversation that the real figure was seven million.[56] And there was another problem: inflation. In 1986, inflation in Vietnam had risen to 582 percent.[57] Skyrocketing inflation had a dramatic impact on people's lives, as Mio Tadashi notes: "Since monthly salaries provided no more than a week's living expenses, almost all households had to find extra sources of income to make up the shortage. It became common in Hanoi for families to use one room of their apartment house units to raise pigs. Pig-farming was the best source of extra income and most families turned one room of a three-room apartment over to pigs, hardening themselves against the noise, odor, and poor hygienic conditions."[58]

Life in Vietnam in the 1980s

Nguyen Trong Hoa taught Russian in Vietnam in the 1980s. He remembers the time vividly: "I still have my savings book from 1984, it has around 100 đ`ông. I lived frugally, poorly to save money, but then, in 1985, the government changed the currency and the book was useless, I couldn't change my money. Life was hard. 1985 was the worst, when people were forced to eat hard wheat, *Hạt bo bo* (bougainvillea seeds), and received aid from Socialist countries such as Russia, Czechoslovakia, and Poland [...]. Average people had 15 kg of rice, the police and soldiers had 21 kg of rice, but it was stored rice, it wasn't tasty, it was dry: 1 kg of fresh rice from the village could be exchanged for 2 kg of stored rice. People normally gave stored rice to their pigs, but city people who were poor had to eat stored rice. It smelled musty. At that time, people with children tried to find fresh rice to cook for their babies. The parents only ate stored rice. We had to make sacrifices for the good of our children. For clothes, you had to use your stamp to get a piece of fabric, which you then had to turn into an item of clothing. My family was hungry, there were only a few pieces of meat each month, we mostly ate rice and vegetables."[59]

From 1985 to 1986, Nguyen Trong Hoa was in Russia, where life seemed much better to him. "I went to Russia in 1985–1986 and, to be honest, at that time, if you went to a foreign country, it was a life changing opportunity, like escaping from hell. If you had the chance to go to the German Democratic Republic, to East Berlin, it was like going to heaven."[60]

But not everyone from Vietnam was so enamored of life in Russia. Nguyen Quoc Minh-Quang, born in 1962, was sent to the Soviet Union as a worker from 1982 to 1988. He remembers working in a factory that produced batteries: "There were so many hardships: the living environment was different, such as the weather, I found it to be extremely cold; the work involved industrial production lines, with machines. It was very new for Vietnamese employees. I had to work eight hours a day, sometimes there weren't any days off at all. Because the factory had its own electrical network, the machines had to run non-stop, so we had to separate our shifts and took turns day and night. The work was quite damaging to my health, it was very toxic because it required me to get involved with chemicals. My salary was only enough for me to scrape by day-to-day. I couldn't save, I had to trade stuff to earn more money."[61]

Even civil servants, who may have earned better salaries, often lived in poor conditions: Vu Dinh Loc, born in 1936, worked as a civil servant and remembers the 1980s as follows: "In 1980, my salary wasn't even enough for one person to live on, but I still had to take care of my family. It wasn't low, but I had to scrape by every day. My salary was 80 đồng, still higher than many people. I was provided 13 kg of rice a month for my family but it wasn't enough, we had to eat corn, bread [...]. Clothing was also limited; I only had a few meters of fabric. At that time, business wasn't allowed. Although I lived in a house opposite Dong Xuan market, I couldn't do any business. So, my parents could only open a sidewalk tea stall in front of our house, and used rainwater to brew tea. Their income wasn't much. When it came to shopping, I couldn't buy anything other than food. I didn't have a refrigerator. To cook, I only had a kerosene stove. There weren't any televisions, we listened to public speakers for news and music."[62]

Vu Dinh Loc and his family shared a house with two other families: "We shared a kitchen, a bathroom, and a yard. There was only one water meter and one electric meter so my family and other families had to work it all out for ourselves and put what money we could aside to pay our share of the bills. Not to mention the differences in personalities, thinking, and opinion. Because of that, there were so many quarrels and annoying situations. My wife and I usually borrowed our salary before payday to be able to pay for stuff, and then we paid it back. Days were hard but, luckily, we didn't have to skip any meals."[63]

When high inflation was added to these modest living conditions, the mood became volatile and criticism of the party grew louder. Although Vietnam was a one-party state, the party leadership was very aware of the shift in public opinion, as we know today from confidential documents.[64]

The Sixth Party Congress and the *Doi Moi* Reforms

The Vietnamese—both the population as well as the party—realized in the mid-1980s that they were at a dead end. Doubts about the Soviet model continued to grow. In April 1986, an economist from Vietnam's Central Institute for Economic Management Research declared that the Soviet model was no longer the only one to follow, but that countries like South Korea could also be taken as an example.[65] The party had been in the grip of a dispute between a faction of reformers and a group that was more suspicious of major change. These two blocs tussled as control of the party went back and forth between them. As mentioned, the first reforms were introduced in the late 1970s, but these were followed by a period in which reforms were frozen. At the Fifth

Party Congress in March 1982 those opposed to further reforms were in the ascendancy.

But the country's problems became ever more pressing, and gradually the pro-reform forces prevailed. At the Tenth Plenum of the Fifth Central Committee in May 1986, the reformers secured a clear victory. Deputy Prime Minister To Huu and others opposed to the reforms lost their seats on the Council of Ministers. In July, Le Duan, the party's General Secretary, died and was replaced by a moderate reformer, Truong Chinh. The new General Secretary was radically self-critical at the Sixth Party Congress and accused the party of committing mistakes such as "idealism, leftist infantilism, subjectivism, and impatience." He criticized the hasty collectivization and the elimination of the private sector.[66] Truong Chinh, however, only remained in office for a short time and was soon succeeded by Nguyen Van Linh.

At the Sixth Party Congress in December 1986, there were large numbers of representatives from the South of Vietnam who supported free-market reforms, such as Vo Van Kiet and Mao Chi Tho. As Balazs Szalontai points out in a paper in *The Journal of Asiatic Studies*, "After all, in post-1975 South Vietnam, despite the imposition of the Communist system, the private sector was by no means eliminated as thoroughly as in the North, and some cadres were willing to harness its potential for growth."[67]

The Party Congress elected Nguyen Van Linh as its new General Secretary. He was born in the North but had fought as a National Front guerrilla for the liberation of South Vietnam during the Vietnam War and had spent most of his life in the South. He was a compromise candidate agreed upon by the two most important factions, the reformers and the traditionalists, explains Balazs Szalontai: "A skilled tactician, Linh had done his best to show his outward respect for the incumbent general secretary,

Truong Chinh, but he also gained substantial popularity in the South by promising to correct the regime's recent 'mistakes.'"[68]

The Sixth Party Congress is regarded as a seminal event in Vietnam's history and the beginning of the fundamental reforms that came to be known as *Doi Moi* (Renewal), which have been the basis for all the positive changes that have occurred in Vietnam ever since.

The party congress was marked by an outpouring of radical self-criticism. In a speech at the congress, a delegate openly stated: "The people have lost faith in the party. This has never happened since the party was founded."[69]

The official report, for the first time, dispensed with a detailed description of the long, heroic struggle of the Vietnamese people and contained only the briefest enumeration of the party and the country's successes. A comparison of various drafts with the final version of the report that was presented at the Party Congress shows that a self-critical view increasingly prevailed: "the first draft concluded that the party line was correct, but that some guidance errors were made in its guidance for implementation, which resulted in half-success and half-failure [...]. However, in the course of discussing the draft, major changes were made in the framework, and it was decided that the emphasis must be placed on the close examination of the subjective deficiencies. As a result, the actual report given at the Congress emphasized at the beginning that they 'must not only ascertain the achieved success, but also earnestly examine the weaknesses, analyze closely the errors and mistakes, clarify their causes, and set new tasks and goals.' The emphasis was on the analysis of the subjective cause that brought about difficulties."[70] What was meant were the mistakes made by the party.

The party leadership openly admitted that the years 1976–1980 were lost years in which there had been effectively no economic growth. The average annual growth rates in the industrial sector were given as 0.6 percent and in national income 0.4 percent. According to Claudia Pfeifer, "In the following Five-Year Plan period from 1981 to 1985, improvements were achieved, but in many cases, this really only meant having restored things to where everything had started in 1975."[71]

The report bluntly addressed numerous issues, including:

- The growth of manufacturing output was not enough to satisfy the needs of the population
- Labor productivity was in decline
- Natural resources were being wasted and the environment damaged
- Inflation was too high
- Unemployment and part-time employment were running in the millions
- The most basic material and cultural needs of the population were not being met
- Law and order were being violated, and corruption was widespread[72]

It says much for the Vietnamese that they did not try to blame external factors, such as the long war with the US and its associated destruction, the military conflicts with China and Cambodia, natural disasters, and so on, for the dire situation their country found itself in. Rather, the final resolution of the Party Congress was decidedly self-critical: "Without underestimating the objective difficulties, the Party Congress comes to the realization that the subjective reasons for the current situation are to be sought above all in mistakes and errors of leadership and direction by the Party and the state."[73]

It also speaks for the Vietnamese that they drew the right political lessons: in essence, the reforms agreed at the Party

Congress and advanced over the next few years focused on giving more freedom to the market and pushing back the all-powerful state. This did not mean a sudden shift from a state-planned economy to a free-market economy. But up to that point, according to socialist doctrine, everything had been based on the state economy, and now the official guideline was that the state, the cooperative, and the private sectors should coexist on an equal footing.[74] Private ownership of the means of production was no longer frowned upon and there was a desire to open up to capitalist foreign countries.

The new political and economic direction also meant that wealth and the rich in society were valued differently. In China, Deng Xiaoping's economic reforms began with the slogan "Let some people get rich first!" At the Sixth Party Congress of the Communist Party of Vietnam, one of the speakers remarked: "We should not be afraid of people becoming affluent, as our country will be strong only when our people are affluent."[75] In his analysis of the Sixth Party Congress, Furuta Motoo writes: "This remark is symbolic of the switch-over from the 'socialism of sharing poverty' to the 'socialism of rewarding life,' and this Congress, by clearly upholding the necessity of a turnabout, set the major basic direction of the reform which was launched as a countermeasure to the crises in 1979."[76]

Once the new reforms had been announced, many Vietnamese were initially skeptical: "Vietnam's history makes its people leery of trends and new forces," write Nancy K. Napier and Dau Thuy Ha. "The last century alone brought French colonialism, communism in 1945, reunification in 1975, and shock in 1989, when trading and political brothers in Russia and Central Europe disappeared. At each twist, the Vietnamese survived, partly by keeping mindsets and ways of acting that had worked for ages: persistence and resourcefulness, stubbornness and cunning."[77]

The announcements were followed by action, even if not immediately. The agricultural production cooperatives were effectively dissolved by largely freeing the farmers to plan production, purchase, and market their products.

In 1988, the reforms began to gain momentum. Important changes included:[78]

- permission for private manufacturers to employ up to ten workers (later increased)
- abolition of internal customs checkpoints
- elimination of the state foreign-trade monopoly
- reduced restrictions on private enterprise
- elimination of virtually all direct subsidies and price controls
- separation of central banking from commercial banking
- dismantling major elements of the central planning and price bureaucracies
- the return of businesses in the South that had been nationalized in 1975 to their former owners or relatives
- the return of land to previous owners in the South if "illegally or arbitrarily appropriated" in the earlier collectivization campaign.[79]

Similar to China, Vietnam's leaders did not try to implement a new system from the top down in one fell swoop, but started with experiments at the local level, and where these were successful, they were transferred to the state level.[80] As Tran Thi Anh-Dao notes: "It was regional experimentation beyond what was allowed by the rules that built up a policy consensus at party headquarters."[81]

One focus of the reforms was agriculture. It is well worth remembering that in 1987, 70 percent of Vietnamese workers were working in agriculture and the sector generated 41 percent of the country's gross domestic product.[82] By 2010, this had already fallen to 53.9 and 20.6 percent respectively.[83] In 2019, 37 percent of the population was still employed in agriculture,[84] and in 2021, the sector generated only 12.6 percent of gross domestic product.[85]

In order to promote private enterprise in the countryside, family farmers were given the right to lease land from cooperative and state farms on a long-term basis at the end of 1987. These farmers' rights of disposal over land were expanded in the 1992 Constitution and the 1993 Land Act. Although land could not be bought and sold as private property, the transferability and inheritability of land on long-term leases (up to seventy-five years) was guaranteed.[86]

The character of the agricultural cooperatives changed. After the collectives were dissolved, farmers now joined together voluntarily. The new cooperatives became service providers that offered certain services to the farmers, much more cheaply than the collectives had done in socialist times. Their services became both better and cheaper at the same time.[87]

In the industrial sector, too, enterprises enjoyed a significantly greater autonomy. The ability of the state headquarters to directly intervene in economic activity at the grassroots level was to be restricted. Economic relations between the enterprises were now to be regulated by mutual contracts.[88] The planned economy was not abolished, but planning now only meant setting strategic goals over extended timeframes. In March 1988, a "Law on the People's Own Industrial Enterprise" was passed. As Claudia Pfeifer explains, "It enabled enterprises to carry out independent production and trade activities, including foreign trade activities."[89]

The setting of wages and the exploitation of profits was now a matter for the individual enterprises and no longer for state planning authorities, writes Claudia Pfeifer: "Enterprises were even granted the right to sell, lend, or rent out capacities that could not be used by the enterprise at a specific moment in time."[90]

In such cases, however, the business's assets remained state property. Subsidies for state-owned enterprises were reduced so that they were forced to work more efficiently. In addition, they had to compete in the market with realistic prices. Many smaller, locally run enterprises that had previously been economically unviable had to file for bankruptcy and, overall, the number of employees in state-owned enterprises fell by about 30 percent (more than 800,000 employees) between 1989 and 1992.[91]

There was no great tidal wave of privatizations, as in some Eastern European countries, since Vietnam followed a similar path to Poland: state-owned enterprises remained, but declined in significance in relation to the private economy. At the same time, the private sector was encouraged by decisions of March and November 1988. Previously, there had been no private enterprises in Vietnam, apart from family businesses, which however were not allowed to employ wage labor—at least officially. Tam T.T. Nguyen notes that, "Under the umbrella of the state-controlled cooperatives, however, there were enterprises that were run as quasi-private enterprises even in the times of the planned economy. This is especially true in the south of the country, where a number of enterprises that had been nationalized in 1975 and 1976 continued as cooperatives under the management of the old owners."[92]

A decisive step under the latest reforms was that private companies were now allowed to hire as many workers as they wanted or needed.[93] Then, in 1990–91, the legal structures of sole proprietorship, limited liability company, and public limited company were introduced.[94] The development culminated in 1992 with Article 21 of the new constitution guaranteeing the protection of private ownership of the means of production against expropriation.[95]

As early as 1987, the introduction of a new investment law sent a clear signal: Vietnam was ready to open up to foreign investors. The new law allowed investments with 100 percent foreign ownership, and Vietnam guaranteed that the capital and property of foreign investors would be safe: it could not be requisitioned, confiscated, or nationalized.[96]

Up until March 1989, the state had fixed all prices. Now, such regulations applied only to electricity, petrol, cement, steel, and transport services. This liberalization of prices led to an improvement in the supply of goods. Although many prices continued to rise sharply, the increases were usually below 100 percent. As late as 1986, price increases had often reached 600 percent. In the case of basic foodstuffs, prices actually remained stable, and in the case of rice, they fell by up to 30 percent.[97]

Even though the beginning of the reforms is dated 1986, as we have shown they started earlier, and by no means ended in the 1980s. Rather, the reforms were an ongoing process. In May 1999, a new Enterprise Law was passed, which further removed bureaucratic hurdles for private companies. As Bill Hayton, expert on the geopolitics of Southeast Asia, sees it, "The impact, once it came into effect on 1 January 2000, was almost instantaneous: over the following five years 160,000 enterprises were registered. Most of these were existing businesses which had been operating without licenses and took advantage of the new law to register. However, the law meant the private sector had finally arrived in Vietnam, twenty years after the start of economic reform."[98]

As important and decisive as the reforms at the Sixth Party Congress had been, it should not be forgotten that they originated in spontaneous, grassroots developments in favor of a freer market, which were then sanctioned at the Party Congress: "For the most part, the reform was in fact a belated authorization of people's 'gray' or 'black' activities."[99]

The new policy direction was accompanied by a new beginning in terms of personnel, and not only at the top. At the Sixth Party Congress, a total of 173 members and candidates were elected to the party's Central Committee, eighty-one of whom (47 percent) were entirely new members.[100] When you consider that 43 percent of the members of the Central Committee at the Fifth Party Congress were newcomers,[101] then it becomes clear just how radical this new beginning was.

Opening Up to the Outside World—Vietnam Benefits from Globalization

The reformers realized early on that the country could only recover if it opened up to the outside world. This "opening up" had a very real and tangible impact on everyday life in Vietnam, as the following report from Lam Duc Hung, a medical doctor born in 1939, shows: "Before *Doi Moi*, the health sector faced many challenges. In the hospitals, the patients only wore dirty clothes, the mattresses were full of lice and bedbugs. Doctors and nurses ate rice mixed with peanuts and corn. Medical equipment and medicines were very scarce."

Between 1981 and 1983, Lam Duc Hung was sent to Algeria on a fact-finding mission. After he came back, he had the task of designing a series of health projects:

> The first project in 1985 was to fight against hospital degradation. I submitted a sixty-page proposal. Initially, the project was not approved. They thought that I would not be able to replicate in Vietnam what had been achieved in Algeria. But it wasn't until 1986, after *Doi Moi*, that a new way of thinking emerged. I was

allowed to announce the project at a nationwide press conference, which attracted international attention. The government immediately provided a total of ten billion d'ồng for hospitals, of which two billion d'ồng was allocated to Bach Mai Hospital where I worked.

Some of my projects after that were Essential Medicines (1988) and UNICEF's Anti-Goiter Program (1989). From 1990–1995, my projects focused on tuberculosis, leprosy, malaria, and other conditions.

Thanks to *Doi Moi* and the open-door policy, multilateral cooperation also flourished. I worked with the Japanese International Cooperation Agency (JICA) to manage new investments in Bach Mai Hospital in 1988–1989. I remember the funds totaled twenty billion dollars and the donors included Japan, Sweden, Italy, and France. Thanks to that investment, we have a spacious and modern hospital. And the hospital food improved, everything was cleaner, and the mood among doctors and nurses got better.

Then there was the machinery and equipment. Thanks to the efforts of my team, JICA invested in Viet Xo Hospital and provided a full suite of imaging tests, including a CT scanner. We were also able to exchange experts and attend international conferences on a more regular basis. For example, I attended seminars in Indonesia in 1989, a seminar about goiter in Bangkok in 1990, and a seminar about primary health care in the Philippines.

Also, thanks to *Doi Moi*, I was able to contribute more and enjoyed greater freedom in my research. It also became easier for me to share my knowledge and expertise. When I was in Algeria, I was struck by the high level of support nurses provided to doctors. That inspired me to establish the Vietnam Nurses Association, which helped to raise the profile of the nursing profession. So, I not only treated patients, I also helped the overall standard of medical care in Vietnam.[102]

The opening up of Vietnam also meant, above all, welcoming foreign investment to the country and integration into the capitalist world economy. In 1989, a Foreign Investment Law was passed and the first investments started to flow into Vietnam from Western Europe, Singapore, South Korea, Thailand, Hong Kong, Japan, Australia, and other countries.

Until the reforms began, the state dominated every aspect of Vietnam's foreign trade, which was mainly with the socialist countries, first and foremost with the Soviet Union. In 1990, the USSR was no longer able or willing to support other socialist states. In the introduction to *Reinventing Vietnamese Socialism: Doi Moi in Comparative Perspective*, William S. Turley, who has been researching Vietnamese communism since 1970, explains: "After years of covering 25–30 percent of its state budget with foreign aid, Vietnam suddenly, in 1991, had to make do with just 5 percent of its revenues from this source."[103]

One of the most important reforms involved the abolition of the system of central-planning specifications and letting companies increasingly manage their own exports and imports.[104] The private import and export of goods was allowed and, in almost no time at all, Vietnam succeeded in compensating for its lost trade with socialist countries by increasing its trade volumes with capitalist countries, especially in Asia (Taiwan, South Korea, Hong Kong, Singapore, Japan) and Australia.

Since the early 1990s, the integration of Vietnam into the global world economy has, according to the World Bank, been "the key driver of Vietnam's outstanding economic outcomes by encouraging competition and a market-friendly business environment."[105]

Over the next few years, trade with China, the US, and Europe was expanded. In 1993, the US lifted its economic embargo, and in 2001 Hanoi concluded a Bilateral Trade Agreement (BTA) with

Washington. "This trade agreement with the US represented a real breakthrough for Vietnam," recalls the German attorney Dr. Oliver Massmann, who has lived in Hanoi for twenty-five years and was instrumental in formulating this agreement. The BTA covers trade in goods and services, intellectual property protection, investment protection, ease of doing business, and transparency safeguards.

"The BTA is the most comprehensive trade agreement Vietnam has signed to date," announced the US.[106] Dr. Massmann recalls: "The negotiations took almost five years, but they ended with a 140-page document that quickly led to a breakthrough for trade between the US and Vietnam." The agreement was signed on December 10, 2001 and, a decade later, the Vietnamese could proudly proclaim: "Over the past ten years, the volume of trade between the US and Vietnam has grown by 1,200 percent, from $1.5 billion to more than $20 billion."[107]

Massmann describes negotiating the trade agreement as an important learning experience for Vietnam and as a prerequisite for joining the World Trade Organization (WTO) in early 2007. "The trade agreement with the US was the breakthrough. Without this trade agreement, Vietnam's accession to the World Trade Organization would not have happened so quickly," explains the attorney.

"Vietnam's accession to the WTO paved the way for the country's entry into the global economy, with bilateral and multilateral FTAs. This membership opened a new chapter in which FDI grew, trade relations expanded, and integration into the global economic map intensified."[108]

All of this had an impact on Vietnam itself, as the WTO agreements also affect national law, with member states committing themselves to align their national laws with the WTO's rules. Vietnam is now a member of all major international economic organizations and institutions, including the Association of South East Asian Nations, the Asian Free Trade Area, the Asia-Pacific Economic Cooperation forum, the World Bank, and the International Monetary Fund.

A free-trade agreement with the EU came into effect on August 1, 2020. The agreement served to remove tariffs, red tape, and other obstacles that European companies faced when exporting to Vietnam. It facilitated trade in key goods such as electronics, food, and pharmaceuticals, and opened Vietnam's market to service exports from the EU, for example, in the transport and telecommunications sectors. Vietnam abolished 65 percent of its tariffs on EU goods on the day the agreement came into force. The remaining tariffs are to be phased out by 2030. The EU will phase out its tariffs on imports from Vietnam by 2027.

On June 30, 2020, another important bilateral agreement between the EU and Vietnam, the EU-Vietnam Investment Protection Agreement (EVIPA), was signed in Hanoi. The EVIPA has to be ratified by all EU member states to take effect. Up to now, only twelve EU countries have ratified the deal. Once the EVIPA takes effect, it will replace all existing bilateral investment agreements between Vietnam and EU member states. These rules will ensure that EU investors will be entitled to the best available treatment. "With the EVIPA," says Massmann, "Vietnam will have a better position than China in attracting more high-quality investment from the EU."

Another important system is the "Investor-to-State Dispute Settlement" mechanism. In disputes regarding investments, the mechanism allows investors to bring their dispute to the Investment Tribunal for settlement. To ensure the fairness and independence of the dispute settlement, the permanent tribunal is composed of nine members: three nationals each appointed from the EU and Vietnam, together with three nationals appointed from other countries. Cases are heard by a three-member tribunal randomly selected by the chairman of the tribunal. The EVIPA also allows for cases to be heard by a sole tribunal member where the claimant is a small or medium-sized enterprise, or the claim for compensation of damage is relatively low. In case either of the disputing parties disagrees with the decision of the tribunal, it can lodge an appeal with an Appeal Tribunal.

For five years after the EVIPA comes into force, any final settlement must be implemented by Vietnam's domestic courts. For the first time in Vietnamese legal history, such settlements will be directly enforceable in Vietnam. After five years, any final settlement will automatically be enforced in Vietnam or the EU country of the investor/state in question. Massmann says: "This IPA will create unmatched levels of legal certainty and bankability in Vietnam."

Today, the Vietnamese economy is "one of the most open to world trade."[109] Vietnam's incredible economic growth proves how nonsensical anti-globalization activists are when they argue that globalization means exploiting developing countries and robbing them of opportunities. The opposite is true. The standard of living in Vietnam has improved—just as it has in South Korea and China, for example—because these countries have benefited immeasurably from global trade. Admittedly, a strong focus on exports, as is typical for countries like Germany, South Korea, and Poland, is not only an opportunity, it can also become a risk if the global economy deteriorates.

Opening up to the outside world also meant opening up to foreign direct investment (FDI). Vietnam has been attracting investors since the 1990s, first from the Asian Tiger economies and Japan, and now also from Europe and the US. Foreign direct investments increased from $7.6 billion to $16.1 billion in the period from 2009 to 2019.[110]

Fund manager Andy Ho highlights the following as the main reasons for investing in Vietnam:

- Vietnam's large population of almost 100 million people, two-thirds of whom are below the age of thirty-five. "It's the last significantly sized market in Asia to develop."[111]
- A rapidly expanding middle class of close to thirty million people.
- The brisk rate of urbanization, which fuels demand for real estate and infrastructure.
- A growing manufacturing sector "that is quickly transforming into the production hub of Southeast Asia thanks to low wages and a reasonably well-educated workforce."[112]
- Stable general conditions (politics, currency, etc.).
- A government committed to continuous economic reforms and full integration into the world economy.

In a study published in 2011, Mai Anh Hoang summarized the findings of several empirical studies on the impact of FDI on growth in Vietnam. Four different studies covering the period from 1988 to 2003 found that: "FDI contributes significantly to economic growth and stimulates domestic investment."[113] However, she herself arrived at a different conclusion, saying "there is no convincing evidence to suggest that openness has been the main engine of economic growth during the last decades."[114] At the same time, she qualified her own findings by stating that "this does not imply that openness does not play an important role in the Vietnamese economy. It is likely that openness has played a very important role in pushing the economy to exploit its comparative advantages and it has promoted competition, enhancing domestic efficiency, especially domestic investment."[115]

In February 2021, the Thirteenth Party Congress of the Communist Party adopted a ten-year economic strategy to shift foreign investment into high-tech industries and to ensure environmental safeguards for these investments. The U.S. Department of State offered the following assessment: "On January 1, 2021, Vietnam's Securities Law and new Labor Code Law, which the National Assembly originally approved in 2019, came into force. The Securities Law formally states the government's intention to remove foreign ownership limits for investments in most industries. The new Labor Code includes several updated provisions including greater contract flexibility, formal recognition of a greater part of the workforce, and allowing workers to join independent workers' rights organizations, though key implementing decrees remain pending. On June 17, 2020, Vietnam passed a revised Law of Investment and a new Public-Private Partnership Law, both designed to encourage foreign investment into large infrastructure projects, reduce the burden on the government to finance such projects, and increase linkages between foreign investors and the Vietnamese private sector."[116]

Foreign investment has also had a key role to play in raising living standards, because salaries and working conditions in foreign-owned companies are often better than those in Vietnamese enterprises. As researchers at the World Bank noted: "Foreign direct investment was important in transforming jobs since most jobs in foreign-owned enterprises are formal, with higher wages compared to domestic firm."[117] Practically every worker in companies owned by foreign investors has an employment contract. In privately owned Vietnamese companies this is true for only one in two workers. Moreover, foreign firms pay workers about twice as much as domestic firms. "Thus, there is a strong correlation between injections of FDI, the increasing number of manufacturing jobs, and higher wages," notes the World Bank 2022 Report.[118]

How the Reforms Have Improved People's Everyday Lives

The reforms worked. But, of course, it took time for a market economy to establish itself and for the effects to become visible to all. Conditions only improved slowly. In the 1980s and into the early 1990s, most people in Vietnam were living in poverty. There was no radical upswing in living conditions. As Vu Dinh Loc reports about this era:

> When my wife retired in 1987, we had some savings, so she wanted to start a business. Even though *Doi Moi* had started at that time, I was scared of losing my job. My friend, a general director of the Central Bee Honey Company, was allowed to start a second business alongside exporting honey, so he started to produce beverages and let us be his authorized distributor with 5 percent of sales. So, we didn't have to contribute to the set-up costs, we only had to redecorate our store, which was part of our home. Our business did great at the time, the containers delivered products to us several times a week. When *Tet* [the Vietnamese Lunar New Year and most important annual festival] came, people queued to buy our alcohol. Then we came up with an idea that we should buy wrapping paper to decorate the bottles in order to charge an even higher price.
>
> In 1989, another company let us be its authorized distributor, so we started to sell paint, lacquer [...]. And then we also sold Bat Trang ceramics. They sold fairly well. But my house was too small so I had to sleep next to the ceramics, on a wooden bed. I had to drive an old motorbike to Bat Trang village (sixteen kilometers from my house) to order new ceramics. I still worked as an officer eight hours a day from Monday to Saturday, then at night I had to deliver ceramics to customers at Nuoc Ngam bus station. Things got better for us.[119]

Many people had to adapt to the new conditions. Nguyen Trong Hoa used to teach Russian, but in the 1990s, nobody really needed to learn the language anymore. He started teaching Vietnamese and set up his own small business as a side occupation—first taking wedding photographs and then operating a copy shop:

> In 1994, I bought a camera and video recorder to start a business as a wedding photographer. I spent 800–900 dollars. One day, my father introduced me to a teacher, who recommended that I should buy a photocopier. So, I bought an old Japanese machine and started my business. I still taught from 7:00 a.m. to 11:00 a.m. I woke up early, started the photocopier, my wife stacked the copies, my daughter stamped them, then the whole family went to work and to school at 7:30. At noon, when I got home, I carried on making copies. That machine took care of my family for two years. In 1996, my wife and I graduated from English class and we officially taught Vietnamese. My daughter went to university, so we sold the machine, which had helped my family to overcome the hardship of that time.
>
> I was allowed to teach Vietnamese to foreigners, so my income increased a lot [...]. In 1996 the policy was totally open, so I could teach whomever I liked. I taught officers from the French, US, and Danish embassies, who would then introduce me to other people. The difference after *Doi Moi* is that I was able to work more freely; before the reforms, I wasn't allowed to teach everywhere, I was only allowed to teach in governmental offices. But after *Doi Moi*, from 1996 onward, I was allowed to teach anyone who needed teaching. I was a Russian language teacher but, at that time, nobody wanted to learn Russian so I switched to teaching Vietnamese to foreigners. In the summer of 1996, I joined a Vietnamese Advanced Summer Institute program (VASI), which

sent students to Vietnam to learn Vietnamese. That was from June
to September. In 1999 one student asked me whether I would
be interested in going to the US to teach, so I asked them how I
could make that happen and they said they would recommend me
and I had to use the internet to connect with the US. I registered
in 2000 but got rejected. Then, in 2002, a US foundation agreed
to invite me to the US to teach. After that, I went to China and
Cambodia. My income was pretty good. After 2000, I was sent
abroad to America. From 2005–2007, I taught Vietnamese in
China. My university had asked me to be a Vietnamese linguist
in Guilin (China). My salary was good.[120]

Nguyen Thi Quat was born in Bac Ninh in 1938, but lived most
of her life in Hanoi. She shares just how much her life changed
after the reforms:

When *Doi Moi* started in 1986, I opened a store in my home. It
was so small, but it was enough for me to sell baby clothes. And
some people even asked me to sell the clothes that they got from
redeeming their stamps. My income rose at that time; we could
eat and live happily. We could have chicken for dinner, unlike
before. Previously, we had only been able to afford meat once or
twice a month. And I remembered that the streets, the people, had
changed noticeably. Incomes had improved for almost everyone
around me thanks to the opportunity of doing business. After
that, we sold clothes for adults, too.

Moreover, I could totally see the rising demand of Vietnamese
people around me. My family was very busy with the store. We
even welcomed some customers at 6:00 a.m. because they traveled
from other provinces just to buy from our store. Sometimes, we
couldn't eat lunch because the store was still crowded at lunch-
time and the same often also happened at dinnertime. There

were no weekends for us, to be honest. The needs of consumers skyrocketed. In 1991, we even had to hire five to six employees for our store. In 1992, my daughter had to stay at home to help us manage the store after she graduated.

A funny story is that before *Doi Moi* we had to eat rice mixed with corn, but when we were able to eat pure white rice, it felt strange and I couldn't get used to it. After years of doing business, we were able to renovate our home. Our daughter even got a Peugeot bike, and my husband had enough money to buy a motorbike. Everything changed drastically. In just ten years, the country had a new look and feel about it. It felt like a turning point for the country.

My stores had become bigger and bigger, and the source of products had become very diverse. We had items from China, Hai Phong, and Nam Dinh. Sewing factories began to appear and connect with us. Our stores had a large amount of domestic products. At that time, Kham Thien Street had a lot of sewing stores, so they provided us with their products. We had a good run of doing business and closed our store in 2010.[121]

Nguyen Quoc Minh-Quang describes how the opening up of Vietnam's economy created new business opportunities for him and thus improved his life:

In 1995, I rented a kiosk on Hang Dao Street to sell products from Thailand. I got a lot of customers. Because of the open-door policy, it was quite easy for us to do business. Hang Ngang–Hang Dao Street became a destination for wholesalers. To me, it was like the trading center for the whole Northern region, everyone flooded to this place to buy and sell. The best season for us traders was a few months before *Tet*. That was the best time of year for us all.

In 1997, I decided to buy a kiosk in Dong Xuan market, to

sell clothes wholesale. China started to open up, their products flooded into Vietnam. I bought goods via a trader in China and resold them. But because there was an intermediary, I couldn't earn much. So, I started to go to Guangzhou myself, went to the factories to buy goods and bring them back to Vietnam. After a while, my wife and I started to make our own products. My wife also went to the Soviet Union as a worker in the garment sector. She designed the clothes and then we went to China to get them produced. We had to finish the designs in May, then I would bring them to China and discuss the costs with the factory. They had to finish producing them before August so we could have them here in Hanoi in September to start selling for *Tet* season. To go to China like that, I had to spend five million d`ông, which equated to about two months of the average salary at the time. But it was worth it because our products sold so well that it had become our own signature. And we had to hire at least two more people to help us with our business. So many wholesale customers came to our kiosk so I think they must have sold very well too. Sometimes, our products just arrived at the transit warehouse, they hadn't arrived at our kiosk yet, but our regular customers had already taken them and paid us later, they weren't even sure if the quality was good or not. The funny thing is, there was a sweater that I wanted to keep for myself but my customer told me to take it off so that he could sell it. Well, I could totally see that demand was rising because people had achieved financial stability in their lives and were now starting to shop to treat themselves. The business was doing so great that we could buy a car and houses. Now, my wife still sells in Dong Xuan market and I switched to the real estate sector.[122]

In the first years of the reforms, progress was slow, and in 1989, three years after the Party Congress had approved the reform agenda, Vietnam's economy was still in serious difficulty, Mai Anh Hoang reports: "Therefore, in March 1989, Vietnam adopted a radical and comprehensive reform package, aimed at stabilizing and opening the economy as well as enhancing freedom of choice for economic units and competition so as to change fundamentally the economic management system in Vietnam."[123]

The results materialized over the next few years: Vietnam's gross domestic product grew by 7.9 percent a year between 1990 and 1996, faster than any other Asian country, with the exception of China, where growth was even higher at 10 percent.[124]

One positive impact of the *Doi Moi* reforms was that poverty in Vietnam fell sharply. There are various World Bank indicators for measuring poverty. The indicator for extreme poverty on a global scale is $1.90/day 2011PPP-IPL (2011 Purchasing Power Parity - International Poverty Line). Accordingly, 52.3 percent of the Vietnamese population was living in extreme poverty in 1993; by 2008, the figure had fallen to 14.1 percent, and by 2020 it was only 1 percent.[125] However, this indicator was developed for "low-income economies," which no longer applies to Vietnam.

Vietnam now belongs to the "lower-middle-income" category of countries, for which the poverty rate is measured at $3.20/day 2011PPP-LMIC (2011 Purchasing Power Parity - Low- and Middle-Income Countries). By this measure, almost 80 percent of the Vietnamese population was living in poverty in 1993, but by 2006 the rate had already fallen to 50.6 percent. By 2020, it stood at just 5 percent.[126]

Life expectancy has also risen sharply in Vietnam as a result of the improved economic situation and the reduction of poverty. In 1980, life expectancy was sixty-two years; today it is 73.6 years (on average, men live to the age of 71.1 and women to 78.2).[127]

Vietnam has also risen in the United Nations' Human Development Index, which claims to comprehensively measure the quality of life of people in a country. The index score for Vietnam increased from 0.463 in 1980 to 0.704 in 2020.[128] This puts Vietnam only slightly below the global average of 0.723 for the 185 countries in the index.[129]

Analyzing the evidence of poverty reduction in Vietnam, a 2022 analysis by the World Bank states:

- "Growth over the last decade in Vietnam was broadly inclusive, as welfare improved across the entire economic distribution of households. Pathways out of poverty were widespread across most groups, as many families moved out of poverty within a single generation."[130]
- "Rising wages, an increasing share of formal employment, and movement out of low-productivity agriculture raised labor incomes."[131]

Despite these major advances, the fight against poverty in Vietnam is by no means over. In particular, there remain a number of significant challenges in relation to rural areas and ethnic minorities. While the poverty rate for the Kinh majority in Vietnam was close to zero in 2020, it was still 27 percent for ethnic minorities.[132]

There has been a fundamental shift in the structure of Vietnamese society. Most people used to belong to the lower class, today most belong to the middle class. The scale of this shift is evident from the following data: in 1998, 71.4 percent of people in Vietnam belonged to the lowest class (in rural areas, the figure was as high as 79.5 percent). In 2008, this had fallen to 50.7 percent, and in 2018, only 24 percent were still considered to be members of the lowest class. The middle class, which had comprised only 27.2 percent of the Vietnamese population in 1998, had risen to 65.4 percent in the same period. And the upper class, which had comprised only 1.3 percent in 1998, had grown to 10.6 percent by 2018.[133]

Inequality also rose during this period, which is what always happens when people escape poverty, as the Nobel laureate Angus Deaton has demonstrated.[134] And Vietnam is no exception: poverty decreased dramatically while inequality, measured in the difference between the income of the lower and upper classes, increased. The income-difference coefficient between the upper and lower classes, which had been 30.3 in 1998, rose to 35 in 2008, and 36.8 in 2018.[135]

From 2010 to 2020, the average household consumption per capita for the lowest 10 percent of the population in Vietnam increased from 7.4 to 12.1 million đ`ông per month. For the richest 10 percent, it increased more, from 52.9 to 136 million đ`ông a month.[136]

But rising inequality is not an issue for the Vietnamese; they view it as a sign of greater justice. In this context, there is a very interesting essay by the Vietnamese social scientists Nguyen Trong Chuan, Nguyen Minh Luan, and Le Huu Tang in the book *Socioeconomic Renovation in Viet Nam*, the content of which I would like to present in detail here. "In previous times under the bureaucratic subsidy system," they write, "justice and equality were construed to have the same meaning. Equality was understood as meaning that people in society are on a par with each other in all respects: politically, economically, and culturally."[137]

In their essay, which they wrote together with researchers from Canada's UBC University, the authors—renowned Vietnamese philosophers and sociologists—oppose equating the concepts of equality and justice. The effects of this egalitarian ideology, they are convinced, have been harmful for the country: "Anything not in accord with egalitarianism would be seen as a violation of the justice principle. This wrongful view decreased, even abolished, momentum for socioeconomic development."[138]

Like classical liberals, they argue that equality should only refer to equality before the law, not to social or economic equality. And social justice cannot mean making everyone equal, but only "that the same contribution equals the same benefit."[139]

In terms of inequality in the rural population, the authors write: "Those households who have good opportunities, better experience, talent for working and trading, and healthy labour, will be richer. Thus, the polarization does not represent inequity but equity: Those who work hard and well will earn more, while those who are lazy and work inefficiently and ineffectively will earn less."[140]

And the authors make it clear that they decidedly oppose proposals for redistribution: "In comparison with the subsidy system, where distribution was egalitarian, the current polarization between the rich and the poor shows the reestablishment of social equity. It is not a sign of the violation of social equity and especially is not a serious violation, as some people claim."[141]

Inequality, they assert, is not worthy of criticism and the pursuit of wealth should be promoted: "Polarization has itself become an important motivating force behind the recent considerable economic growth. Therefore, now is the time for us to promote the results already obtained, and to encourage people to enrich themselves legally. It is not appropriate to stop this evolution because of the existence of the polarization between the rich and the poor."[142]

The authors cite the results of surveys conducted in 1993 and 1994, six to seven years after the *Doi Moi* reforms began. The results show that "in Quangnam-Danang Province, 91.2 percent of 663 households considered the current polarization between the rich and the poor to be normal and acceptable." In HôChí

Minh City, the percentage of respondents who considered the polarization between rich and poor to be "normal and acceptable" was 72.9 percent, and in Hanoi it was 80.2 percent.[143]

These Vietnamese sociologists and philosophers conclude that it would be wrong to abandon the course of free-market reforms just because inequality between rich and poor is increasing. "In other words, although the polarization between the rich and the poor becomes more and more evident, this does not mean that we should stop encouraging people's legal enrichment."[144]

You would be hard pressed to find similar statements from sociologists in the US or Europe. In Western countries, social inequality is almost always regarded negatively and proposals to combat poverty are mostly aimed at closing the "gap between rich and poor" via even more extensive redistribution measures.

Adding to the positives, social mobility clearly works in Vietnam. A study showed that between 2016 and 2018 alone, one-third of the population experienced such large income changes that they moved to a different social class: 12.6 percent of households moved down during this period, but many more, 21.4 percent, managed to move up the social ladder.[145]

The contrast between the findings of the Vietnamese scholars quoted above and anti-capitalists from the West could not be greater. Günter Giesenfeld quotes the Belgian Marxist sociologist (and Catholic priest) François Houtart, who directed the following criticism at developments in Vietnam: "Social polarization is intensifying. A new social class is emerging that benefits from the conversion of the economy and can afford to consume." He calls them "nouveau riche," and brands them greedy, "red capitalists."[146] He laments that "not only does the disintegration and disappearance of the social safety net rob individuals and families of any remaining security in planning their lives, but moreover the unleashing of economic mechanisms causes a deepening of differences and a sharpening of antagonisms." The sociologist draws a negative conclusion: "There is no longer a single project within society that can quicken spirits, galvanize energies, and endow social life with collective meaning. Yes, there are many reasons for this, but what is certain is that the promises of the market deal a final blow to the construction of a society based on solidarity, disperse energies, and narrow horizons."[147]

This criticism shows that left-wing, anti-capitalist intellectuals in the West are suspicious of Vietnam's reforms, even though they have lifted so many millions of people out of poverty. But even though the living standards of ordinary people in Vietnam have greatly improved, this is of no consequence to anti-capitalist intellectuals as long as it means saying goodbye to their utopian notions of a "society of solidarity" that would give people "collective meaning."

Findings of a Survey on the *Doi Moi* Reforms

In Vietnam, I commissioned the Vietnamese polling institute Indochina Research to conduct telephone interviews with a total of 800 representatively selected people from October 19 to November 7, 2022. In our survey we wanted to know, among other things: "In your opinion, how much impact have the *Doi Moi* reforms had on your financial situation? Would you say your financial situation has been impacted by the *Doi Moi* reforms a lot, somewhat, hardly or not at all?" More than two-thirds of Vietnamese (68 percent) said that the reforms have had an impact on their financial situation and only 24 percent said they had not (Figure 3.1).

Figure 3.1   Vietnam: Impact of the *Doi Moi* Reforms on Respondents' Own Financial Situations

Question: "In your opinion, how much impact have the *Doi Moi* reforms had on your financial situation? Would you say, your financial situation has been impacted by the *Doi Moi* reforms a lot, somewhat, hardly, or not at all?"

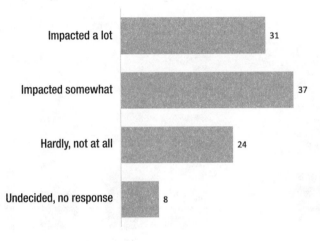

Source: Indochina Research

Among respondents over the age of sixty, namely those respondents who are best placed to judge the impact of the reforms (those born in 1961 were twenty-five years old when the *Doi Moi* reforms began) as many as three-quarters (75 percent) say the reforms have had an impact on their lives, and half in this age group (49 percent) say their personal financial situation has been impacted "a lot." As the age of our respondents increases, so does the strength of their assessment of the impact of the *Doi Moi* reforms on their own financial situation, as shown in Figure 3.2.

Figure 3.2   Vietnam: Impact of the *Doi Moi* Reforms on Respondents' Own Financial Situations. Analysis by Age Group.

Question: "In your opinion, how much impact have the *Doi Moi* reforms had on your financial situation? Would you say, your financial situation has been impacted by the *Doi Moi* reforms a lot, somewhat, hardly, or not at all?"

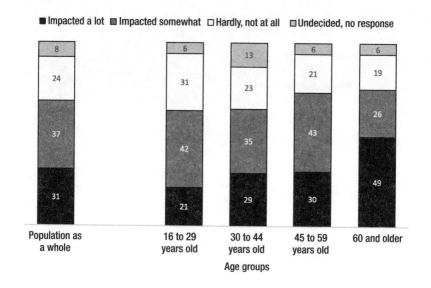

Source: Indochina Research

Women in Vietnam Play an Important Role

Another aspect of inequality is the imbalances that exist between the sexes. In a representative survey I conducted in Vietnam and twelve other countries (see Figure 3.3 on page 93), I noticed that in all countries men were more likely than women to say that it was important to them to become rich. It was only in Vietnam that significantly more women than men want to become rich: 72 percent of men and 80 percent of women in Vietnam said in the survey that it was important to them to become rich.[148]

In Hanoi, I spoke with Dinh Tuan Minh, the representative of a private think-tank. He emphasized the major contribution that women make to Vietnam's economy. According to a survey by

Grant Thornton in 2019, 36 percent of executives in Vietnam are women, compared to 19 percent in Thailand. In my home country, Germany, the figure is 29 percent.[149] In a profile of Vietnam, the *Neue Zürcher Zeitung*, the leading Swiss quality broadsheet, wrote: "Unlike women in other Southeast Asian countries, the door to all professions and management levels is wide open for Vietnamese women."[150]

In Hanoi, I gave lectures at several universities, including the renowned NEU (National Economics University) and the Foreign Trade University. At the Foreign Trade University, I was invited to a workshop on the motivation to become rich. The workshop motto: "Rich people, rich country." The Foreign Trade University has 20,000 students, two-thirds of whom are female. The university has 850 faculty and staff members, and according to the university, the proportion of women is even higher.

In Vietnam, all of this has been achieved without feminist ideology. I spoke with the entrepreneur Nguyen Xuan in Hanoi and she had the following to say: "In Vietnam, it's less about demanding rights for women and more about doing something yourself to succeed as a woman. We don't want to rely on men, we want to rely on ourselves." This is something I had observed from previous visits to China: Asians, who are supposedly "collectivist" from a European perspective, are much more individualistic in this respect than Europeans and Americans. They don't think you should expect the state to do something for you, they believe you should do it yourself.

Xuan herself is a good example: she started her first company, a chain of sandwich restaurants (similar to Subway), when she was only twenty-three. She now owns twelve eateries in Vietnam and twenty in the South Korean capital, Seoul. Once her restaurant chain was up and running, she started a chain of pharmacies and, three years ago, a publishing house for audio books, which has already published 700 titles.

Today, Vietnam is home to seven billionaires. This wealthy circle is still dominated by men, but there is at last one woman among them: Nguyen Thi Phuong-Thao (in the US, in comparison, there is only one woman among the twenty richest individuals, Alice Walton, and she is an heiress). Nguyen Thi Phuong-Thao was born in 1970 and is among the 1,400 richest people in the world, with a fortune of $2.1 billion, according to *Forbes* (October 2023). She earned her first million at the age of twenty-one as a student in Moscow by selling fax machines. In 2011, she founded the low-cost airline VietJet Air. She had a great affinity for marketing from day one. In 2012, her airline hit the headlines with commercials that showed flight attendants in bikinis. Flight attendants could choose whether they preferred to fly in traditional uniforms or bikinis, and most opted for the latter. Nguyen Thi Phuong-Thao says she has no problem with people associating her company with bikini stewardesses: "If that makes people happy, then we are happy."[151] In response to allegations that this turns women into sex symbols, she says: "If a beautiful image helps our customers feel happy, we will always try our best. In this world, there are a lot of beauty contests where the contestants wear bikinis [...]. The bikini shows beautiful characteristics. Our message at Viet-Jet is we did this for the benefit of beauty and happiness."[152] In 2017, her Saigon-based company went public and she became a billionaire. In addition, the entrepreneur is active in the banking sector (HD Bank) and has also invested in real estate, including owning three beach resorts.

Investment fund manager Andy Ho, who invests in equities and buys direct stakes in companies in Vietnam (private equity), reports in his 2021 book *Crossing the Street: How to Make a Success of Investing in Vietnam,* "Many of Vietnam's top businesses are headed by women. Although I have not done a formal study of how the country compares to others, I would have to say that women lead more large companies in Vietnam than in most others."[153]

He cites several examples of large and very successful companies in Vietnam that have female leaders. He has had very positive experiences with private-equity investments in such companies: "These women have all been extremely effective in raising capital and growing their businesses. A common theme is that even when they bring in investors, they continue to hold significant stakes in the companies they run—their interests remain aligned with other shareholders. Most of all, they have remained focused, even after their companies have grown and become successful."[154]

With men, on the other hand, Ho says they often spend too much time gambling, golfing, or having affairs once they have become successful. Maintaining a mistress in Vietnam easily costs $5,000 a month, and men are distracted from their business activities, he says.[155] "Although I am an equal opportunity investor, I will admit to having a higher level of confidence in companies run by women, at least until they give me reason otherwise."[156]

Room for Improvement: The Problems of State-Owned Enterprises and Corruption

Despite the incredible successes, there remains much work to be done in Vietnam. One problem is that there are still too many state-owned enterprises, and they often operate inefficiently. In 2020, the Asian Development Bank Institute analyzed the problems related to state-owned enterprises (SEOs). First, some figures: "It is worth noting, although the number of SOEs only accounts for 0.4 percent of the total number of enterprises, they make up 28.8 percent of the whole country's capital, contributing 20 percent of the country's GDP."[157]

Most private companies in Vietnam are small; 97 percent have fewer than ten employees, while state-owned enterprises tend to be very large.[158] Although SOEs receive preferential treatment when it comes to getting loans and in many other respects, the data prove that they operate less efficiently and less profitably than private enterprises. The authors of the analysis draw attention to this contradiction: "they [the SOEs] receive a large number of incentives in access to land, credit, and information that are not eligible to private-owned enterprises, namely preferential financing treatment, loan guarantees, public procurement advantages, and better informational access. Therefore, poor performance in SOEs is not always rational and understandable." And yet, many Vietnamese state-owned enterprises are active in lucrative sectors where there is a lot of money to be made, such as banking, and food and beverages.[159]

However, the supposed contradiction that the authors point out is, in my opinion, in no way an incongruity: it is precisely *because* state-owned enterprises receive higher subsidies, *because* they are often not exposed to fierce competition and, above all, *because* they do not simply go bankrupt when they operate uneconomically, that they perform so poorly. This is confirmed by the following figure: "SOEs comprise 17 percent of outstanding debt in the economy but they are responsible for 60 percent of non-performing loans."[160] At the same time, the return on equity ratio for SOEs is only half that of foreign companies that invest in the country.[161]

The Vietnamese government avoids the term "privatization" in relation to state-owned enterprises and prefers to speak of "equitization." And this process is faltering. Between 2003 and 2006, a total of 2,649 state-owned enterprises were "equitized," but since then the number has been in the low three-digit or even double-digit range every year.[162] The privatizations have included a number of very large state-owned enterprises such as Vietcombank, the large beverage company Habeco and the beer brewery Sabeco. The problem, however, is that in most cases the state has retained majority stakes in such companies.[163] Statistics on the equitization of ten large enterprises from 2005 to 2011 show that the state retained more than 90 percent of the shares in seven of these ten companies and gave up more than 50 percent in only one (the construction company Covesco).

Some state-owned enterprises that had failed in their original business fields, or were extremely unprofitable, were forced to change their business models in order to survive at all. They took advantage of their ownership of land and access to cheap state loans in order to gain a footing in the real estate or hotel business, for example.[164]

Privatization is probably faltering for several reasons: first, many state-owned enterprises do not operate efficiently enough, so there is little incentive for private investors to acquire them. Additionally, if the government insists on retaining a controlling stake in the company, investors suspect that the bureaucrats won't be relinquishing their control anytime soon. Moreover, it is simply a question of motives: the leaders of state-owned enterprises belong to the party and have little interest in their companies being privatized. The state is still active in economic sectors where it is absolutely implausible as to why this should be the case, such as shipbuilding and tobacco production.

Often there were and still are massive conflicts of interest in state-owned enterprises, as investor Andy Ho explains with an example: "One of my first investments in Vietnam was in a fish-processing company that had recently equitized, with the government still the majority shareholder. Upon visiting the plant in the Mekong Delta, it became clear to us that more than half of the inputs (raw fish) came from the fish farms owned by the families of SOE executives. As such, the CEO was always able to guarantee a 10 percent gross margin! Needless to say, we had no comfort around the SOE's ability to purchase inputs at the lowest possible price, and I asked my team to exit the business completely."[165]

One problem with the "equitization" process involves the valuation of the companies' assets, "since the assets of many had no market value," as the Australian economist Melanie Beresford writes. Another problem, Beresford explains, is that the directors of state-owned enterprises are worried about losing control and workers are afraid for their jobs as a result of the "equitization" process.[166] Thus, the process remains little more than a half-hearted measure and is not being implemented consistently.

In November 2018, a government-controlled media outlet reported that Prime Minister Nguyen Xuan Phuc had convened a conference on privatization. There was an urgent need for improvement because, the article stated bluntly: "The privatization process is not yet going as expected and therefore needs efficient and timely measures."[167] In her analysis, Melanie Beresford writes: "After the end of central planning, the only remaining element of the earlier definition of socialism in Vietnam was the government's determination to maintain state enterprise domination of the economy's commanding heights."[168] But in practice, the government in Vietnam did not do much to offer state-owned enterprises a promising future, and state-owned enterprises "were largely left out in the cold," notes Beresford. Changing tack, the government started to target its investments at infrastructure projects rather than state-owned enterprises. "Investment in SOEs diminished rapidly, to a small fraction of the total, and relied heavily on short-term credit for working capital rather than long-term investment for structural change and improved efficiency."[169]

The state-owned enterprises found themselves in a peculiar situation: "Market discipline was largely absent, but government discipline was not implemented either [...]. It is clear, however, that the government has persisted in exploring avenues of reform that would enable SOEs to play a dominant role in a 'market economy under state guidance.'"[170]

Beresford takes a rather critical view of this because she argues for the state to take a more active role in the economy. Where Beresford sees a negative, I, however, see a positive, namely that the state started to focus more on promoting private foreign investment than on turning state enterprises into instruments of an active industrial policy: "The main reason for the situation is," writes Beresford, "that the focus of policy and strategy was on institutional reform (enterprise autonomy and regulation by laws) rather than on using industry policy to promote investment in the government's priority development areas. It is hard to avoid the conclusion, when examining the situation of SOEs, that far from using them as instruments of nation building, the Vietnamese state allowed the priorities of the private sector, especially foreign investors, to act as the key determinants of the process."[171]

Besides the excessive number of inefficient state-owned enterprises, corruption is another problem that Vietnam is grappling with. According to Transparency International's Corruption Perceptions Index, Vietnam ranked a middling eighty-seventh out of 180 countries in the 2021 ranking. The index uses a scale that runs from zero for an entirely corruption-free economy to 100 for an economy plagued by the highest possible levels of corruption. Vietnam has improved from seventy-six points in 2003 to sixty-one points in 2021.[172]

During my time in Hanoi, a businessman told me: "The official lists of party and state functionaries' salaries are published in the newspapers, and many only get $500 or $1,000 a month. Nevertheless, they often drive expensive Mercedes and lead lavish lifestyles. Of course, one wonders: where does the money come from?"

A report by the Friedrich Naumann Foundation Hanoi from 2020 states that Vietnam is well-known for its "envelope culture." This, the report says, means that citizens voluntarily or involuntarily pay to receive things from the government or other officials that they are actually entitled to for free by law as taxpayers.

At registry offices, for example, sealed envelopes of cash are handed over in exchange for marriage certificates. Or patients in government hospitals think nothing of giving money to receive necessary injections from nurses or to be treated more quickly. In a survey, 61 percent of citizens said they had paid bribes in return for services in the public sector.[173]

The government frequently launches campaigns against corruption. For example, video cameras have been installed in many offices to film officials at work to prevent them from receiving "envelopes." The video idea originated in Quang Ngai province and was soon taken up elsewhere. In one province, offices were also made literally "transparent" with specially installed windows.

Vietnam's state president (October 2018–April 2021) and party leader Nguyen Phu Trong has waged a campaign against corruption in recent years. So far, thirty-eight senior officials and ministers have been put on trial. The accused included twenty-three generals and a former Politburo member. Prison sentences of between five and thirty years were handed down for bribery, fraud, and extortion. No one was acquitted. A former minister who, according to the court, took a bribe of $3 million was sentenced to death. But the president has not only been praised for his tough campaign. His critics allege that he is using the battle against corruption as a cover to get rid of his political opponents, including those loyal to a former prime minister.[174]

The greater the influence a government has over a country, the more pervasive corruption will be. It is no secret that the former socialist countries were particularly plagued by corruption. The view that corruption is especially prevalent in capitalist countries is wrong. The opposite is true, as confirmed by a comparison of Transparency International's Corruption Perceptions Index CPI with the Index of Economic Freedom. The countries with the lowest levels of corruption also happen to have the highest levels of economic freedom. The ten countries with the lowest levels of corruption are all, without exception, in the Index of Economic Freedom's "free" or "mostly free" categories: Singapore, Denmark, Finland, New Zealand, Switzerland, and the Netherlands are among the ten most corruption-free countries in the world—and they are all among the ten most economically free countries!

Conversely, countries in the bottom ten of the Corruption Perceptions Index are also classed as "repressed" in the Index of Economic Freedom. The two worst performers in the Index of Economic Freedom, Venezuela and North Korea, are also among the worst performers in the Corruption Perceptions Index. The more the state intervenes in economic life, the greater the opportunities to bribe government officials. Anyone who wants to limit the wealthy exerting unethical or even criminal influence on the political agenda should therefore not advocate for bigger, but for smaller government.

Even though Vietnam has created more space for the market since the *Doi Moi* reforms and the government is no longer as omnipotent in the economy as it was in socialist times, the party still retains a great deal of influence. That, logically, gives rise to the question: To what extent is it really possible to effectively fight corruption in a one-party system without a free press?

Vietnam: Economic Reform—But One-Party Rule

In 1986, the year in which the *Doi Moi* reforms were launched in Vietnam, Mikhail Gorbachev also started to implement his policy of *perestroika* (reconstruction, transformation, restructuring) in the Soviet Union. He wanted to reform and modernize the Soviet system. Nguyen Van Linh, elected General Secretary of the Communist Party of Vietnam at the end of 1986, was even referred to as "Vietnam's Gorbachev" in the first years after his election.[175] Nguyen Van Linh said that the Sixth Party Congress, which is considered the beginning of the *Doi Moi* reforms, was inspired by the Twenty-Seventh Party Congress of the CPSU.[176] That was the party congress at which Gorbachev had promoted his reform policy of *perestroika* and *glasnost* (openness, transparency).

In December 1988, an article appeared in the Vietnamese army's official newspaper, *Quan Doi Nhan Dan*, which stated: "We have declared in documents, resolutions, and speeches our endeavor to renovate the political system, but in reality, the same old system continues to exist with all of its fundamental characteristics intact."[177] The article quoted passages from Gorbachev's speeches at great length and praised his reforms as a model against which Vietnam's reforms should be measured.[178]

But the influence of Gorbachev's policy of *glasnost* and *perestroika* should not be overestimated. As a senior official of the Communist Party of Vietnam remarked, "for the Vietnamese the greatest benefit of *perestroika* was that they no longer felt bound by the doctrines of Communist (i.e., Soviet) ideology." Vietnam, he said, should decide for itself how to solve its economic problems.[179] In addition, the Vietnamese began to take a greater interest in the reforms initiated in China a few years earlier by Deng Xiaoping. For example, in July 1986, Hanoi asked if they could send a delegation of thirty bureaucrats on a fact-finding trip to study the impact of the economic reforms in China.[180]

As Vietnam was preparing to launch its own program of reforms, both the Chinese reforms under Deng Xiaoping and Gorbachev's reforms in the Soviet Union were models that were discussed. "Until the dramatic transformations of late 1989 in the Soviet Union and Eastern Europe, Vietnam's leaders described their reforms as combining the best of the Chinese and Soviet approaches. While China focused on economic reforms and slighted political reforms, the Soviet reforms did not sufficiently emphasize the economic dimension. Hanoi's leaders regarded themselves as having a more satisfactory balance between politics and economics."[181]

However, the Chinese experience was not the only one that served as a point of orientation. So did that of South Vietnam, which had had a market economy before reunification that had even partly survived the communist era. The party's bureaucrats understood that they could learn from the entrepreneurial experience in South Vietnam.[182]

In the first phase of the *Doi Moi* reforms, efforts were made to introduce political reforms along the lines of those in Gorbachev's Soviet Union. The leading role of the Communist Party was not questioned, but the role of other institutions, especially the National Assembly, was to be strengthened. At the Sixth Party Congress in December 1986, the party acknowledged its own shortcomings, as William S. Turley explains in the book *Reinventing Vietnamese Socialism*: "To strengthen the effectiveness of the management by the state means, first and foremost, to uphold the role of the National Assembly and the State Council, and of the People's Council at all levels. At present, people-elected bodies at different levels are still chosen, elected, and functioning in a formalist way. In many cases, Party committees at various levels run the whole show, doing the work of State organs, in many places the selection of people to elected bodies is done in a forcible manner. Many People's Committees do not truly respect the People's Councils."[183]

The party's leaders recognized that there should be a stronger distinction between the state and the party at all levels and that people's participation should be boosted.[184] Under the slogan "leadership by the party, mastery by the people, and management by the state," moves were made to establish a clearer distinction between the function of the party, the state, and elected representatives. This was also evident in the country's "mass organizations," such as trade unions. At the Sixth Trade Union Congress in October 1988, all of the delegates were, for the very first time, elected by local assemblies of members. In the elections for the union's executive committee, 70 percent of the old members were voted out and four-out-of-five independent candidates won. During the meeting there was an open and very critical discussion of the issues.[185]

The rules had also changed for elections to the National Assembly in April 1987. In the previous election, in 1981, only 614 candidates had stood for 496 seats. This time, there were 829 candidates. It is true that the Vietnam Fatherland Front played a major role in nominating candidates in these elections, "but individuals were permitted to nominate themselves and run as independents."[186]

However, the collapse of one-party rule in Eastern European countries gave leaders in Vietnam pause for thought. In Poland, for instance, the communist dictatorship ended with the first free elections in June 1989, from which *Solidarność* (Solidarity) emerged as the leading force. This reminded the communists in Vietnam of the very real risks when economic reforms moved into the field of politics. "By 1989 all of Eastern Europe became more a nightmare for the Vietnamese elite than an object of emulation."[187]

At the same time, there was another event in neighboring China: in Tiananmen Square in Beijing, a student-led movement had been peacefully demonstrating for weeks in the spring of 1989, calling for sweeping political reforms and democracy. On the night of June 4, the Chinese government brought in tanks and bloodily suppressed the democracy movement here and all across the city.

There were two interpretations within the Vietnamese Communist Party as it analyzed what precisely had led to the collapse of socialism in Eastern Europe. Reformers in the party saw above all the mistakes and mismanagement of the communists and their failure to carry out real reforms as the cause. Traditionalists interpreted the collapse as the result of the action of foreign powers and "imperialist sabotage."[188]

General Secretary Nguyen Van Linh managed to combine both interpretations simultaneously in a speech in February 1990. On the one hand, he criticized "errors in economic development, slow improvement of socioeconomic management procedures, despotism, lack of democracy"; on the other, he also bemoaned "violations against Marxist-Leninist principles and the imperialist forces' sabotage activities" as causes of the crises in the former socialist countries.[189]

At the Eighth Plenum of the Central Committee in March 1990, Linh categorically ruled out a "bourgeois liberalization" or "multiparty democracy" for Vietnam, emphasizing above all the need for political stability and the primacy of the party. At the same time, the collapse of the socialist systems in Eastern Europe had made it clear to him that there was no alternative to economic reform. The only options from Nguyen Van Linh's point of view were simply "renew or die."[190]

The guiding principle in Vietnam from then on was "economic renovation is the key task," as articulated by Do Muoi, who was elected as Linh's successor at the Seventh Party Congress.[191]

Relaxations of press restrictions and other political reforms that had been implemented in the early days of *Doi Moi* were reversed and it was stipulated, for example, that newspapers were only allowed to be state-owned.[192]

That the focus was on economic reforms and not on political change was, of course, above all an expression of the party's desire for self-preservation; it did not want to relinquish its power. Moreover, there was a reason that was rarely mentioned explicitly: economic reforms often lead to a temporary deterioration. In many cases, this is only for a brief period, such as two years, as was the case in Poland, but sometimes this phase can last longer. Under the conditions of a multiparty system and a free press, populists and the media take advantage of these teething problems to attack the reforms themselves. This was the bitter lesson the reformer Leszek Balcerowicz was forced to learn in Poland (for more on this, see the next chapter). At best, such attacks lead to the reforms being watered down; at worst they are abandoned. "The predominant (and official) view, which has Confucian as well as Leninist roots, holds that spontaneous participation and multiparty competition would unleash social conflicts and thus interrupt production, transportation, markets and foreign investments, dashing hope for development. This view found its most vociferous expression in 1989, when party leaders concluded that liberalizing reforms in other socialist countries had generated demands that the regimes could not satisfy."[193]

Pragmatism and a Focus on the Present Are the Reasons for Vietnam's Success

If you ask about the underlying reasons for Vietnam's success, it is above all pragmatism and a focus on the present. This pragmatism has its ideological roots in Confucianism. Pragmatism is evident not only in the country's economic reforms, but also in the way the country deals with history and its relationship with America. As the entrepreneur Nguyen Xuan told me: "I was born in 1987, when the war had already been over for twelve years. My parents and grandparents told me about how terrible the war was, but they never had a bad word to say about Americans. On the contrary, they told me, 'You have to learn English, dress like Americans, eat what Americans eat, and above all, learn to think like Americans think. Then you will be successful.'"

In a survey conducted by the Pew Research Center in 2014, 76 percent of Vietnamese respondents said they had a positive view of the US. Among better-educated Vietnamese, the figure was as high as 89 percent, and among respondents aged between eighteen and twenty-nine, as many as 89 percent had a positive view of the US. Even among those over the age of fifty, who had lived through the war, more than 60 percent had a positive view of the US.[194]

I always admire people who manage to look more to the future than to the past. Such people are usually much more successful in life than those who spend most of their time worrying about the past. This is true not only for individuals but also for nations. Many African countries today complain about the consequences of colonialism and use that as an explanation for all their problems today. The Vietnamese could do that just as well, but they don't—they look to the future.

Of course, this does not mean that they ignore history. I visited an impressive memorial in Hanoi, a former prison first used by the French colonists to incarcerate Vietnamese prisoners and later by the North Vietnamese to hold American soldiers. Today, Hoa Lo Prison is a museum. At the time, American prisoners of war ironically referred to the prison as the "The Hanoi Hilton," and a film about the experiences of American prisoners of war there was made under this name in 1987. The prison's inmates included the later presidential candidate John McCain. Today, the exhibition displays photos of his rescue from a lake near Hanoi in 1967 after his fighter plane was shot down. It also documents his visit to the prison museum in 2000.

But even the history of the prison confirms that, if there were any lingering doubt, the present and the future are more important to the Vietnamese than the past. For in the meantime, large parts of the Hoa Lo complex have given way to a gigantic shopping mall, the Hanoi Towers. Ironically, in the 1990s, the American Hilton Group explored buying the vacant lot created by the partial demolition of the original Hoa Lo complex to build the first Hilton hotel in Vietnam. "This venture was criticized by the American press as extremely macabre because of its significant connection to American-Vietnamese history. Then, in 1999, a Hilton Group hotel, the Hilton Hanoi Opera Hotel, actually opened in the Vietnamese capital."[195]

The Japanese researcher Vu Le Thao Chi spent fifteen years studying the health implications of the use of the defoliant Agent Orange, which caused genetic damage to hundreds of thousands of children in Vietnam. She followed eighty families whose disabled children suffered from conditions caused by Agent Orange and was astonished to find "that these parents rarely link their children's misfortune to the principal cause, namely Agent Orange and the war that brought the substance to their backyard. The war seems to have faded into the distant past and with it the link between the cause of their children's misfortune and the war [...]. None of the families, or for that matter the Commune Clinic [where many disabled children were housed] staff brought the operations to our attention, even casually. To them, Agent Orange, like the war itself, is far removed from their life. Anything disruptive needs to be ignored or, if it cannot be ignored, tucked away in comforting narratives that can make light of it."[196]

This does not mean that Vietnam ignores its past. There are countless memorials that commemorate the wars against France and the US, and of course many books and films in Vietnam do the same.[197] For the Communist Party, the war played a key role, because it gave the party the legitimacy it needed to rule the country. After all, the party had led the war of liberation against the French and the Americans. But the party knows that these past merits are not a basis for the loyalty of the people of today, who above all value the economic rise and the victory over poverty in Vietnam.

In his book on the commemorative culture in Vietnam, Andreas Margara emphasizes the fact that the memory of the war plays "only a subordinate role" among the younger generation. Young people want to "consume the future," their gaze is directed toward a promising economic tomorrow and not toward a past marked by deprivation. "*Song voi* (live now), is the *carpe diem* motto of Vietnamese youth. They now regard Americans as their friends. No wonder: the models for the hedonism returning to the cities all come from the West and are called Bill Gates and Steve Jobs. As visible proof of their economic success, the new rich openly display luxury goods, such as smartphones and vehicles."[198]

That Vietnam has changed is not only due to structural reforms, but mainly because attitudes—the national mindset, if you will—have changed, allowing the positive traditions of Confucianism to be combined with a capitalist mentality. "Free to choose" are the words Milton Friedman used to describe the essence of capitalism. In their book *The Bridge Generation of Vietnam*, Nancy K. Napier and Dau Thuy Ha describe how the old recipe of "No Choice Soup" has changed into the new recipe of "Choice Soup" in Vietnam:

1. Start with three teaspoons of Confucian society, including rules about children obeying their parents' instructions on everything from education, to family, to work and marriage.

2. Add three teaspoons of planned-economy principles, including government rules, oversight and direction on production capacity of agricultural, machinery, and educational output.

3. Sprinkle in one teaspoon of mindset of young people who want to do right by their families and country and obey both.

4. Mix well for fifty years.

5. Result: young people who follow rules and don't realize they lack choice.

In contrast, the new recipe is:

1. Begin with five teaspoons of Confucian society and rules about children following their parents' instruction.

2. Toss in one heaped teaspoon of internet and exposure to countries outside the Soviet Bloc.

3. Dilute planned economy broth with 2.5 teaspoons of market-oriented economic principles and remove half of the rules about production capacity and how to earn money.

4. Mix well for ten years.

5. Result: young people who realize they have choices but may not know how to make good ones. Simmer for another ten years. Result: the children of people who transitioned from 'no choice' to 'choice' now make their own decisions with a vengeance.[199]

What People in Vietnam Think of the Rich

Rich people enjoy a very positive image in Vietnam today. In September 2022, I was invited to Hanoi by the Foreign Trade University, which had been looking into my research on attitudes toward the rich. The topic of one of the university's workshops was the image of rich people in Vietnam. At the workshop, I presented the results of a survey I commissioned from the research institute Ipsos MORI on wealth and the image of rich people.

The results appeared in the book *The Rich in Public Opinion*, which was also published in several other countries and in several different languages, including in the United States, Italy, Spain, Sweden, and also in Vietnam. The project began in 2018 with surveys in France, Germany, the UK, and the US, followed by Spain, Italy, Sweden, China, South Korea, Chile, Poland, and Vietnam over the next few years. One particularly interesting result of the survey was that nowhere else is the percentage of people who say that becoming rich is important to them as high as in Vietnam (Figure 3.3).

Figure 3.3　How Important Is It for You Personally to Be Rich?

Question: "For some people, it is important to be rich. How important, if at all, is it for you personally to be rich?"
Answer: "Very important" / "Fairly important"

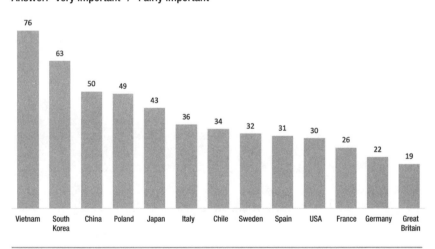

Sources: Allensbach Institute surveys 11085 and 8271, Ipsos MORI surveys J-18-031911-01-02, J-19-01009-29, J-19-01009-47, J-20-091774-05, J-21-041026-01, 22-087515-44, 22-055857-01, and 22-055857-01

In total, Vietnamese respondents were presented with seventeen positive and negative statements about rich people. Agreement with the positive statements about rich people clearly dominated (Figure 3.4).

Figure 3.4   Vietnam: Attitudes Toward the Rich

Question: "Here is a list of things that people have said about rich people. Which, if any, of the statements on the list would you agree with? Please think about people with assets worth at least 10 billion đồng, not including the home, they live in."[200]

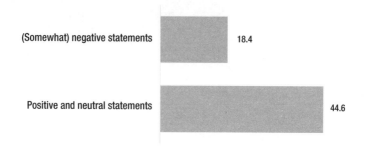

Source: Ipsos MORI survey J-21-041026-01

The Vietnamese think that the rich become rich mainly because they are willing to take more risks (62 percent), because they have special skills and ideas (58 percent), and because they are particularly industrious (57 percent). At the same time, 60 percent regard rich people who have made it on their own as role models (Figure 3.5).

Negative statements about the rich elicited far less support among the Vietnamese. Most of the negative answers met with the approval of pretty much exactly one-fifth of the respondents, so that one can conclude that about one-fifth of the Vietnamese have a negative attitude toward the rich (Figure 3.6).

Figure 3.5   Vietnam: Attitudes Toward the Rich—Positive and Neutral Statements

Question: "Here is a list of things that people have said about rich people. Which, if any, of the statements on the list would you agree with? Please think about people with assets worth at least 10 billion đồng, not including the home they live in."

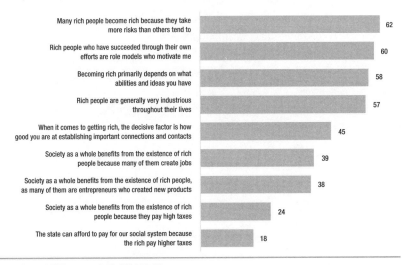

Source: Ipsos MORI survey J-21-041026-01

Figure 3.6   Vietnam: Attitudes Toward the Rich—(Somewhat) Negative Statements

Question: "Here is a list of things that people have said about rich people. Which, if any, of the statements on the list would you agree with? Please think about people with assets worth at least 10 billion đồng, not including the home they live in."

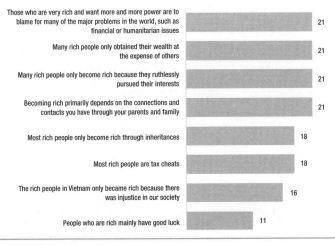

Source: Ipsos MORI survey J-21-041026-01

Figure 3.7 Vietnam: Personality Traits Attributed to the Rich

Question: "Which, if any, of the following are most likely to apply to rich people?"

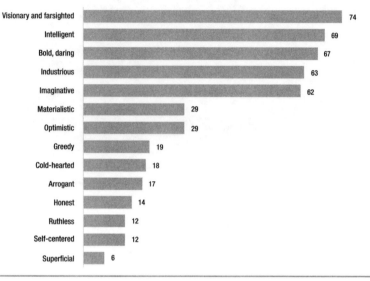

Source: Ipsos MORI survey J-21-041026-01

Ipsos MORI also asked which personality traits Vietnamese people thought were particularly common among the rich (Figure 3.7).

In none of the other thirteen countries where we conducted the survey in this form were positive personality traits selected so frequently (54 percent on average) and negative ones so rarely (16 percent on average). It follows that the so-called Personality Trait Coefficient (PTC) is lower in Vietnam than anywhere else (the lower the coefficient, the more frequently positive personality traits are attributed to the rich: see Figure 3.8).

Figure 3.8 Personality Trait Coefficient (PTC) in Thirteen Countries

Note: The lower the coefficient, the more positive the personality traits attributed to the rich.

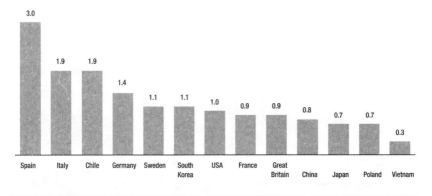

Sources: Allensbach Institute surveys 11085 and 8271, Ipsos MORI surveys J18-031911-01-02, J-19-01009-29, J-19-01009-47 J-20-091774-05 and 22-055857-01

What do people in Vietnam think about taxes on the rich? In all countries, most respondents agree that the rich should pay higher taxes than those on lower incomes. But *how* high should taxes be for the rich? We gave respondents two alternatives to choose from:

A. The taxes on the rich should be high, but not excessively high, because they have generally worked hard to earn their wealth, and the state should not take too much away from them.

B. The rich should not only pay high taxes, but they should pay very high taxes. In this way, the state can ensure that the gap between the rich and the poor does not become too great here in our country.

Responses to these two statements in Vietnam are surprisingly clear: 63 percent say that taxes on the rich should not be excessively high and only 21 percent advocate very high taxes on

Figure 3.9: High Taxes on the Rich? Popular Opinions in Thirteen Countries

Question: "On balance, which, if any, of the following statements do you agree with MOST?"

▨ Taxes on the rich should be high but not excessively high

■ The rich should not only pay high taxes, but they should pay very high taxes

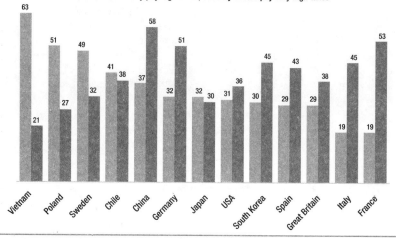

Sources: Allensbach Institute survey 11085, Ipsos MORI surveys J18-031911-01-02, J-19-01009-29, J-19-01009-47, and J-20-091774-05

the rich. In most other countries (with the exceptions of Poland and Sweden), respondents see things differently; majorities in these countries are in favor of extremely high taxes on the rich. Nowhere was opposition to high taxes on the rich as strong as in Vietnam, followed by Poland (Figure 3.9).

The survey also asked several questions designed to measure the extent of social envy against the rich in each country (for the methodology, please see pages 160–162 of my book *The Rich in Public Opinion*). In Vietnam, the Social Envy Coefficient was low at 0.43, about the same level as in the US. By combining the Social Envy Coefficient (triple weighted) and the Personality Trait Coefficient (single weighted), we arrive at the Rich Sentiment Index (RSI), which allows us to make an overall comparison of how people in a given country feel toward the rich. The result: it is only in Poland that attitudes toward the rich are slightly more

Figure 3.10 Rich Sentiment Index RSI in Thirteen Countries

The lower the number, the more positive the attitude toward the rich

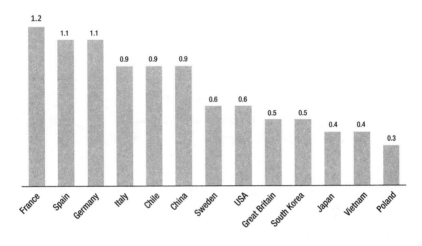

Sources: Allensbach Institute survey 11085, Ipsos MORI surveys J18-031911-01-02, J-19-01009-29, J-19-01009-47, and J-20-091774-05

positive than in Vietnam, while attitudes in Japan are at the same positive level (Figure 3.10).

What People in Vietnam Think of Capitalism

From June 2021 to November 2022, Ipsos MORI conducted a survey on my behalf in thirty-three countries to find out what people in different nations feel about capitalism and the market economy. In Vietnam, the public-opinion research institute Indochina Research conducted a representative telephone survey of 800 people between October 19 and November 7, 2022.

This survey differs from many other surveys on capitalism not only in its depth (i.e., in the level of detail of the questions asked), but also in a particular method: the hypothesis before the survey began was that some people are repelled by the word 'capitalism' in particular, even though their actual views would put them more in the pro-capitalist camp. There could be a number of reasons for this: some people have only vague and unclear associations with 'capitalism,' others connect the term with all of the evils of this world. Thus, one set of questions (on economic freedom) consistently and deliberately avoided the word 'capitalism.' Respondents were presented with a total of six statements, of which three statements favored economic freedom and a market economy, and three advocated a strong role for the state. The set of questions on economic freedom included, for example, the statement: "We need a lot more state intervention in the economy, since the market fails time and again." Another, in contrast, stated: "I am for an economic system in which the state sets the rules but ideally does not interfere otherwise." For each country, we calculated the average levels of support for the "pro–economic freedom" and the "pro–state intervention" items and used these data to calculate how people in any given country feel about economic freedom.

In Vietnam, an analysis of responses to the three pro-state and three pro-market statements reveals that statements in favor of a stronger role for the government meet with 79 percent approval, compared with 61 percent approval for pro-market statements in favor of greater market freedom. Dividing the average of positive statements by the average of negative statements yields a coefficient of 0.78. We will come back to this coefficient frequently in the next few pages: a coefficient greater than 1.0 means that pro–economic freedom attitudes dominate, a coefficient less than 1.0 means that anti–economic freedom opinions are in the ascendancy.

In contrast, the term 'capitalism' was used in the two other sets of questions. By combining the data for the last two sets of questions, we are able to determine what people think of capitalism when the actual word 'capitalism' is used. It is interesting to compare this with the first set of questions, where the answers reveal how people feel about capitalism when the word is not mentioned. By comparing responses across the three sets of questions, we can see exactly what role the word 'capitalism' plays. In Vietnam, support for capitalism actually *decreases* by 41 percent when the capitalist economic system is described without using the word 'capitalism.' In almost all other countries, approval of capitalism *increases* (in some cases substantially) when capitalism is described without actually mentioning the word. In Vietnam, as our survey data confirms, the word 'capitalism' does not have a bad ring to it; rather, it is loaded with positive connotations.

Respondents were also presented with a list of ten terms, positive and negative, and asked which they associate with 'capitalism.' An average of 65 percent of respondents associate 'capitalism' with negative terms such as "greed," "corruption," and "environmental destruction." In contrast, positive terms such as "prosperity," "progress," "innovation," and "freedom" were selected by 77 percent. This result is astonishing in its clarity: Vietnamese people associate the word 'capitalism' predominantly with positive terms.

In other countries, we tended to find the opposite: approval of the market economy increased in most countries when the word 'capitalism' was not used. In Vietnam, in contrast, people tend to associate 'capitalism' with positive features, such as "progress" (81 percent), "innovation" (80 percent), "a wide range of goods" (77 percent), "prosperity" (74 percent) and "freedom" (71 percent). Negative terms such as "greed" and "corruption" (64 percent each) or "coldness" (55 percent) are selected somewhat less frequently. Nevertheless, two negative terms, "performance-oriented, constant pressure to achieve" (72 percent) and "environmental degradation" (70 percent), are more frequently selected, as depicted in Figure 3.11.

Figure 3.11 Vietnam: Associations with 'Capitalism'

Question: "Please now think about the word capitalism. For each of the following statements, select whether that is something you associate with capitalism."

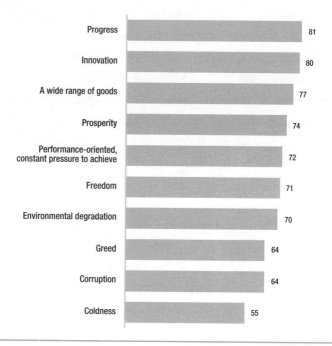

Source: Indochina Research

Respondents were presented with a total of eighteen statements about capitalism, ten of which were negative and eight of which were positive. This set of questions confirms what we have already seen from the association test: Vietnamese people primarily associate capitalism with positive things. In fact, this finding is particularly clear for this set of questions. Of the thirty-three countries surveyed to date, Vietnam is the only one in which the five statements that receive the highest levels of agreement are all pro-capitalist.

In Vietnam, the statement that attracts the most agreement (78 percent) is: "Capitalism means economic freedom." Only in Japan and South Korea did this statement also come in first place, and only in a total of five out of thirty-three countries so far has this statement made it into the top five most supported statements.

The second highest level of agreement, 74 percent, is for the statement: "Capitalism has improved conditions for ordinary people in many countries." In only one other of the thirty-three countries where we have conducted the survey (Nigeria) did this statement rank among the top five. In most countries, significantly more people agreed with the negative statement: "Capitalism is responsible for hunger and poverty." In Germany, for example, only 15 percent said "Capitalism has improved conditions for ordinary people in many countries," while 45 percent said "Capitalism is responsible for hunger and poverty." In Vietnam, the tables are turned: the negative statement that claims "Capitalism is responsible for hunger and poverty" received significantly less support (53 percent) than the positive statement that "Capitalism has improved conditions for ordinary people in many countries" (74 percent).

The statement: "Capitalism encourages people to do their best," which was the third most frequently selected statement in Vietnam, also attracted very strong support (71 percent). Only in three of the thirty-three surveyed countries did this statement make it into the top five.

In fifth place in Vietnam is the statement: "Capitalism ensures prosperity" (64 percent). Again, there is only one other of the thirty-three countries in which this statement also makes it into the top five. In sixth place in Vietnam, we have the statement: "Capitalism may not be ideal, but it is still better than all other systems" (59 percent). The critical opinion that "Capitalism entices people to buy products they don't need," on the other hand, was among the top five in eleven of thirty-two nations. In Vietnam, in contrast, this statement attracted less support than any other of the eighteen statements (23 percent), as shown in Figure 3.12.

Figure 3.12 Vietnam: Eighteen Statements About Capitalism

Question: "Which of the following statements about capitalism, if any, would you agree with?"

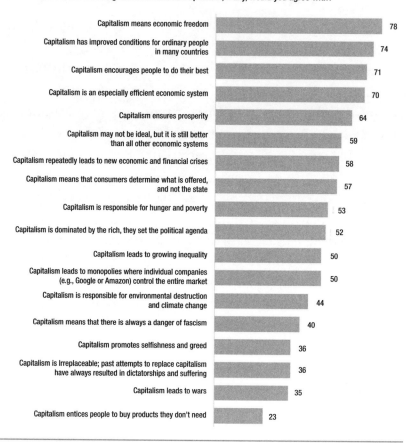

Statement	Value
Capitalism means economic freedom	78
Capitalism has improved conditions for ordinary people in many countries	74
Capitalism encourages people to do their best	71
Capitalism is an especially efficient economic system	70
Capitalism ensures prosperity	64
Capitalism may not be ideal, but it is still better than all other economic systems	59
Capitalism repeatedly leads to new economic and financial crises	58
Capitalism means that consumers determine what is offered, and not the state	57
Capitalism is responsible for hunger and poverty	53
Capitalism is dominated by the rich, they set the political agenda	52
Capitalism leads to growing inequality	50
Capitalism leads to monopolies where individual companies (e.g., Google or Amazon) control the entire market	50
Capitalism is responsible for environmental destruction and climate change	44
Capitalism means that there is always a danger of fascism	40
Capitalism promotes selfishness and greed	36
Capitalism is Irreplaceable; past attempts to replace capitalism have always resulted in dictatorships and suffering	36
Capitalism leads to wars	35
Capitalism entices people to buy products they don't need	23

Source: Indochina Research

The average agreement with pro- and anti-capitalist state-ments was calculated for all three sets of questions and a coef-ficient was calculated by dividing the two averages: this allows us to summarize what the people in a country think of capitalism in a single digit. If we combine the responses to all thirty-four survey items, we see that in only six of thirty-three countries is capitalism viewed more positively than in Vietnam, while in twenty-six countries it has a more negative image (Figure 3.13).

Figure 3.13 Overall Coefficient on Attitudes Toward Capitalism in Thirty-Three Countries

Note: The lower the coefficient, the stronger the anti-capitalist attitude

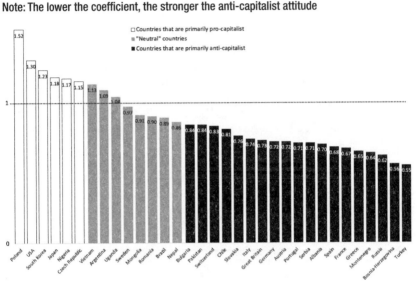

Sources: Allensbach Institute survey 12038, Sant Maral Foundation, Ipsos MORI surveys 20-091774-30, 21-087515-07, 22-014242-04-03 and 22-087515-44, Indochina Research, FACTS Research & Analytics Pvt. Ltd. and Research World International Ltd.

We also wanted to know which economic systems around the world our Vietnamese respondents most admire. So, we asked them whether they have a positive or negative view of the economic systems in the following countries: China, South Korea, North Korea, Japan, Taiwan, France, Singapore, the United States, and Russia.

The clear winners are all capitalist countries: Japan with an approval rating of 82 percent, South Korea with 79 percent, and Singapore with 78 percent. The United States gains 71 percent approval, while Russia receives as high an approval rating as the United States—a result that is difficult to understand given the inefficiency of the Russian economic system.

In contrast, the two countries that describe themselves as socialist (as Vietnam does) receive the lowest levels of approval:

only 40 percent of Vietnamese respondents admire China's economic system, while 55 percent say they disapprove of it. The proportion of respondents who like North Korea's economic system is even lower, at 35 percent, while 38 percent reject it (Figure 3.14).

It is possible, however, that the results partly express general sympathy/antipathy for the countries. For example, we know that the United States, despite the Vietnam War, is generally well regarded in Vietnam, while China has a very negative image. Among young Vietnamese respondents under the age of thirty, the American economic system is actually the second most popular, after Japan, along with South Korea. And approval of the system in North Korea is even lower than in the population as a whole (Figure 3.14).

Although Vietnam calls itself socialist, the population (especially the young) are more closely aligned with capitalist countries such Japan and the US. The people of Vietnam have learned that capitalism is not, as many people in the West believe, responsible for poverty, but quite the opposite—only capitalism helps people to escape poverty. If Vietnam continues to follow its current free-market path and succeeds in implementing the reforms that are still pending, it has a good chance of becoming one of the world's leading economies. However, if Vietnam (like China in recent years) forgets why it has achieved such enormous improvements in living standards and goes back to relying more on the state, it would be squandering a massive opportunity.

Figure 3.14 Vietnam: Which Economic Systems Do the Vietnamese Like?

Question: "When you think of different economic systems from different countries, which one do you like well, and which one do you like less?"

Answer: "I like the economic system of this country."

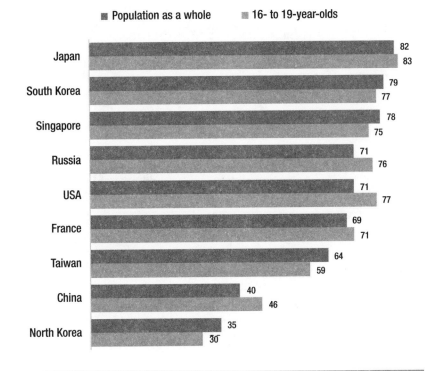

Source: Indochina Research

CHAPTER FOUR

POLAND: RISE OF THE WHITE EAGLE

Standing in line developed into a fully-fledged science in socialist Poland, as Iwona Kienzler explains in her book about everyday life under the rule of the communist workers' party in Poland: with lines everywhere and people often having to wait for hours and hours—or even several days in the case of furniture or household products—some clever systems emerged. One of them was the so-called "line list," which was used when people had to wait for days, not hours. In that case, a list was made of all the people waiting in line so that they didn't need to physically be there all the time. Every several hours the list was read aloud and people needed to report present, or otherwise, if they were no longer in line, they would be crossed off the list. The schedule for taking the register was announced ahead of time. When the waiting period was days not hours, people needed to report three-to-four times a day. Some people took a leave of absence from work, some just asked supervisors to let them go and come back quickly, and some paid others to report on their behalf (it was called "hiring a stander"). Custody over the line list was taken care of by a self-proclaimed line committee.[1]

Let's take another example from the book *80-te. Jak naprawdę żyliśmy w ostatniej dekadzie PRL* [*The 80s. How We Really Lived*

During the Last Decade of the PRL] by Joanna Solska. To shop more effectively, people abused the privileges of pregnant women and women with children: "Shops were often areas of contrast between theoretical and real socialism. In theory the system respected women, and bestowed privileges on those with children or pregnant. One of these privileges was a possibility to shop without waiting in line. So, women with children would come to shops (some would just borrow children from their friends) and go straight to the counter. The greater the shortage of a product, the more women with children would come. While they were buying up all there was to buy, the rest of the people in the line would barely move."[2]

Tomasz Agencki, with whom I produced a film about socialism and capitalism in Poland (*Poland: From Socialism to Prosperity*) also reports on the resourcefulness of the Poles when it came to bartering *in lieu* of conventional purchases. Yes, he says, it was an advantage to know someone who could get you certain products. "But in reality, it was way more layered than that. You had to know the salesperson in a shoe shop, who could sell you a pair of shoes that you would then present as a bribe to a guy that could sell you a bicycle that you would then give to the baker to pay for the wedding cake for your electrician's daughter. This kind of reality is depicted in a number of movies, especially the ones directed by Stanislaw Bareja. There is even a special word in Polish for an absurd situation, *bareism*, that derives from his name."

According to Karl Marx, socialism was nothing more than a transitional stage to communism. Under communism, so his line of reasoning went, all people would be able to live according to their needs. The Poles who stood in line for hours to get the bare necessities of life, however, faced the reality of Marx's vision with derision. One popular joke in Poland was:

"How will the problem of queues in shops be solved when we reach full Communism?"

"There will be nothing left to queue up for."[3]

None of this was all that long ago. The above reports all describe the situation in Poland in the 1980s, which was a world away from today's Poland. Since 1989, Poland's gross domestic product per capita has increased threefold.[4] Poland has recorded average real economic growth of 3.5 percent per year. The country's economy grew to become the sixth-largest in the European Community in the decades following the launch of market-economy reforms.[5] Poland has had the fastest-growing economy in Europe since the 1989 reforms and is widely regarded as "Europe's Growth Champion," which also happens to be the title of a book by Marcin Piatkowski. There is a principal reason for this astonishing growth: in hardly any other country of comparable size has economic freedom increased so much in recent decades.

The Heritage Foundation has been publishing the *Index of Economic Freedom* every year since 1995. Theoretically, the highest achievable score any country could get is 100, but none of the 177 countries analyzed for the index achieves the maximum score (the top performers in 2022 were Singapore and Switzerland at 84.4 and 84.2 points, respectively). Conversely, the lowest theoretical score would be zero, which North Korea comes close to at 3.0. Poland ranks thirty-ninth with a score of 68.7, which does not seem particularly remarkable at first and is certainly not among the highest scores. Nevertheless, it does mean that Poland is more economically free than Spain, Israel, France, or Italy, for example.[6]

But of far greater importance than the absolute rank is a country's relative change since 1995, and on this measure, Poland does come out on top. Poland's score rose from 50.7 in 1995 to 69.7 in 2021. In 2022, Poland lost one point for a score of 68.7.

True, there are some very small countries such as Georgia (3.7 million inhabitants) and Bulgaria (6.9 million inhabitants) that experienced an even greater increase. But of countries with more than thirty million inhabitants, only Vietnam, which rose from 41.7 to 60.6 points, experienced a comparably large increase in economic freedom.[7]

But economic freedom in Poland today is under threat. In particular since 2015, when the PiS party took power, spending on social welfare programs has surged, privatizations have largely been halted, and even banks and businesses that had already been privatized have been transferred back into the hands of the state. Under the PiS government (2015 – 2023), Poland was in the process of abandoning the market- economy path that made the country so successful. Although the latest developments are not yet adequately reflected in the Heritage Foundation's ranking, economic freedom in Poland has declined in recent years. Nevertheless, this does not detract from the success story of Poland in the twenty-five years from 1990 to 2015. But let us tell the story from the beginning and take a journey back to the dark times when Poland experienced a terrible war, the fourth partition of the country, and then a socialist regime.

A Tortured Land

Poland was partitioned three times between Prussia, Russia, and Austria in 1772, 1793, and 1795, and subsequently disappeared entirely from the European map for 123 years after the last of these three partitions. The Second Polish Republic only came into being after the First World War, and managed to survive for just twenty-one years, from 1918 to 1939.

The end of Poland as an independent country was settled in the Hitler-Stalin Pact between National Socialist Germany and the socialist Soviet Union. On August 23, 1939, Germany's Foreign Minister Joachim von Ribbentrop met his Soviet counterpart Vyacheslav Molotov to sign the pact in Moscow, with the partition recorded in a secret additional protocol. In September 1939, first German and then Soviet troops invaded and occupied the country, celebrating their victory in a joint parade on September 22.

The proposal for a joint parade of German and Soviet troops came from the German side. A German camera team was on hand to film the spectacle and their footage of the military parade of Adolf Hitler's and Josef Stalin's troops was a feature of the *Deutsche Wochenschau* newsreels in October 1939.

The two commanders Heinz Wilhelm Guderian and Semyon Moiseevich Krivoshein marched together past a German and a Soviet tank battalion in the center of Brest-Litovsk. A German military orchestra played the national anthems of the two victorious powers. Immediately after the parade, the German troops left the city and a boundary stone was placed to mark the border between the Soviet Union and the German occupied zone.

Germany occupied almost half of Poland, a territory that was home to a population of 21.2 million people. The eastern part of the country, with 13.2 million inhabitants, was occupied by the USSR. According to the Poland expert and political scientist Stefan Garsztecki, the effects of the reign of terror were staggering: "Between five and six million Polish citizens lost their lives, including almost three million Polish Jews. A majority of the victims were civilians (who, moreover, continued to die even after the end of hostilities), shot by *Einsatzgruppen* [mobile task forces], gassed in German death camps such as Auschwitz-Birkenau, Majdanek, Chełmno, Treblinka, Sobibór, and Bełżec, or killed as a result of forced labor, imprisonment, or related hardships. During all of this, it was not only Jews that were the victims of genocide, but also other Poles. The targeted campaigns against the Polish elite, such as the *Sonderaktion Krakau*, directed against professors and academics at universities in German-occupied Kraków, or Heinrich Himmler's speech in Poznań on October 4, 1943 to SS group leaders, in which he said that he was only interested in the peoples of Eastern Europe in so far as they were needed as slaves, demonstrate the genocidal character of German occupation policy in Poland, including against ethnic Poles, just as the General Plan East and *Aktion Reinhardt* did."[8]

The Soviets also unleashed a brutal reign of terror in Poland: during the period from April to May 1940, as many as 15,000 Polish officers, who were held as prisoners-of-war, were murdered in accordance with a decision issued by the Political Bureau of the Central Committee of the Russian Communist Party on March 5, 1940. They were all shot in the back of the head and their bodies were buried in mass graves in Katyń, Kharkov, and Myednoye. As a result of the same edict, 7,000 members of the Polish elite who had been arrested and detained in NKVD prisons were also murdered.

Until such time as the 'Katyń massacre' was revealed by the Germans in 1943, the Polish government had made futile attempts to establish what had happened to those who had disappeared. The Soviets refused to admit the crime, accusing the Germans of having carried out the atrocity. For Poles, the 'Katyń massacre' became synonymous with Soviet genocide and the regime's monstrous lies. Over 320,000 Polish citizens were deported into the depths of the Soviet Union during four waves of mass deportation which took place in February, April and June 1940, and in June 1941. The individual waves of deportation initially applied to "kulaks" ("rich" peasants), military settlers, and forest workers, followed successively by the families of prisoners sentenced to death by the edict of March 5, 1940, refugees from the German occupied zone, and finally the inhabitants of border zones.[9]

But nowhere was resistance to the occupiers as fierce as in Poland, as exemplified by the uprising of Polish Jews in the Warsaw Ghetto on April 19, 1943, and the Warsaw Uprising of August 1, 1944. Warsaw had been home to 1.3 million inhabitants before the war; there were only 350,000 toward the end of the uprising.[10] The Polish capital lost about as many lives to war, occupation, and the Holocaust as the whole of France did during the same period.[11] In total, Poland was left to mourn the deaths of five to six million victims in World War II, according to estimates. Proportionately, the losses were even worse for the elites, whom the German and Russian occupiers sought to wipe out. "Poland's population loss is estimated at 22 percent (the highest of all the countries participating in the war), but it lost 40 percent of its medical doctors, a third of its teachers, scientists, and scholars, and 26 percent of its lawyers."[12]

From February 4 to 11, 1945, the Soviet dictator Josef Stalin, the US President Franklin D. Roosevelt and the British Prime Minister Winston Churchill met in the Soviet seaside resort of Yalta on the Crimean peninsula. With regard to Poland, the allied leaders decided that the Soviet Union should retain possession of part of the eastern territories. The new eastern border of Poland was to be the Curzon Line. Poland was to be compensated for its losses in the east with territorial gains in the north and west at the expense of Germany. However, the final decision on Poland's western border was postponed to a peace conference after the end of the war.

Another tragic chapter in German-Polish history was the expulsion of the Germans from Polish territory. Prime Minister Churchill declared in the British House of Commons in 1944: "Expulsion is the method which, insofar as we have been able to see, will be the most satisfactory and lasting. There will be no mixture of populations to cause endless trouble as in Alsace-Lorraine." Between the end of the war in 1945 and late 1949, millions of Germans were expelled from the territories that had now become Polish and many lost their lives in the process. In total, between eight and nine million Germans left their homes within the new Polish borders after 1944–45 as they fled or were expelled.

The agreements struck between the victorious Allies stipulated that "a strong, free, independent, and democratic Poland" should be established. The other European states were also to be granted the right "to choose the form of government under which they will live." But the reality was very different, as the socialist Soviet Union forced its system on Poland, on Central Germany, which had now become East Germany, and on several Eastern and Central European countries.

The Polish United Workers' Party (PZPR), formed on December 15, 1948 from the union of the Polish Workers' Party (PPR) and the Polish Socialist Party (PPS), helped to achieve this goal. Many members of the PPS opposed this union, but were forced to join the new party. The conference's delegates exalted the Soviet dictator Stalin, the man who, together with Hitler, had agreed to the fourth partition of Poland and had launched the war against it in the first place. But these historical facts did not count now, of course. The delegates passed a manifesto in which the history of the Second World War was rewritten. As Andrzej Friszke and Antoni Dudek explain in their book on the history of Poland between 1939 and 2015, the concept of Poland's "independence" was reinterpreted: "Accordingly, prior to World War II, 'monopoly capitalism' was allegedly the greatest enemy of Polish independence [...]. During the war against 'Hitler's fascism,' the Soviet Union had single-handedly saved the Polish nation from 'physical annihilation.'"[13]

Socialism in Poland

The new political system in Poland was called "people's democracy," which would implement the "dictatorship of the proletariat." In 1946, a referendum was held in which the Poles were asked to settle three issues: the first concerned the abolition of the Senate, the second addressed land reform and the nationalization of companies, and the third dealt with confirming the western border along the Oder and Neisse Rivers. However, the results were falsified. Poland's new rulers proceeded in exactly the same way as they had during the first "elections" of January 1947: supposedly, 80 percent of the electorate voted for the so-called Democratic Bloc (the Communists, Socialists, and other affiliated parties), but there are indications that it was actually the opposition Polish People's Party (PSL) that should have won.[14]

Of the 1,157 members of the *województwa* (provisional) committees in 1953, 61 percent had only completed their primary school education or had no education at all, 70 percent were workers, and 11.5 percent were farmers. Only one percent of the people responsible for the political committees had a university degree.[15] In other words, there were new opportunities for social advancement for workers and peasants, but only if they were loyal to the party line and were deemed to be "ideologically stable." Among the 7,000 people who held leading posts in the economy, 53 percent belonged to the PZPR; among the heads of the central administrative bodies of the economy, 75 percent were party members.[16] As in other now socialist countries, the trade unions were no longer independent representatives of the workers' interests; instead, they served as political instruments to enforce the party's directives among the workers' ranks.

In 1952, a new Polish constitution was drafted by a commission appointed by the party's Central Committee. The new constitution was modeled on the Soviet constitution of 1936, and Stalin personally read the draft document and added some fifty corrections.[17] Stalin made it clear that the Soviet Union was indeed to determine policy in Poland by making a Soviet marshal, Konstantin Rokossovsky, Poland's first defense minister.[18]

As in other socialist countries, a large proportion of enterprises (if they had not already been nationalized in Poland in the pre-war period or during the occupation)[19] were nationalized. Prices were set by a planning authority. Labor productivity in Poland grew only slowly. In the 1950s, it rose by 2.6 percent per annum in Poland. In comparison, growth of 6.6 percent was registered in West Germany over the same period. In the 1960s, productivity grew by 2.1 percent in Poland, and 5.2 percent in West Germany.[20] Moreover, Poland's GDP per capita grew by only 2.2 percent per year during the period of socialism, from 1950 to 1989.[21] Even on the basis of the official Polish figures, which are justifiably questionable, Marcin Piatkowski makes it clear in *Europe's Growth Champion* that "Poland was the European economic laggard."[22] This slow growth was remarkable, especially as, after World War II, Poland was one of the poorest countries in Europe. In Poland, income per capita was only $2,500 per year (in 1990 prices). If anything, such poor countries should grow faster. Here is another comparison: the southern European countries of Spain, Portugal and Greece, which were as poor as Poland in 1950, grew at twice the rate.[23]

The weak growth of the Polish economy is remarkable for another reason: the new territories in the west, in particular the former German territories of Pomerania, Silesia, and southern East Prussia, which Poland had gained, were richer, had better infrastructure, a more developed industrial base, larger cities, and more productive agriculture than those of the eastern territories that Poland was forced to surrender to the Soviet Union.[24]

After World War II, Poland was a largely agrarian country. At first, the Communists tried to implement their methods (which had already failed miserably in the Soviet Union) onto Polish agriculture as well. The wealthier peasants, who were called "kulaks," as they were in the Soviet Union, were branded "exploiters," "spies" and "thieves" by the Communists. Farms larger than fifty hectares were expropriated and divided into small plots. They were given to "small farmers," who were to work on them and shape Poland's agriculture into a new form that better suited the communist ideology. "It seems in retrospect, however, that these actions met with little success, since those 'small peasants' who were to be made the new spokesmen within the village communities seldom met with the approval of the other villagers."[25] The communist policy of collectivization in Poland failed; only a few percent of agricultural land was farmed collectively. Instead, the state tried to enforce levies by exerting massive pressure on the peasants. Between 1952 and 1955 alone, about half a million peasants were arrested for failure to pay compulsory levies.[26]

Economic incentives were replaced by pressure. One important instrument in exerting this pressure was the State Security Service, which had some 33,000 agents in 1953, 90 percent of whom were party members, more than any other state agency. But 18 percent of the State Security agents did not even have a primary school diploma, and only 7 percent had completed high school.[27] "It is estimated that the security organs tried to recruit about half a million people in the years 1944 to 1956. Within society, the view—broadly accurate—spread that 'they are everywhere' and that 'the walls have ears.' By 1954, an internal Ministry personal file of 'suspects' included some six million people, or one-third of Poland's adult population."[28] Anyone who told a politically inopportune joke, did not show up at one of the official factory rallies, or made mistakes at work (which could easily be interpreted as sabotage) knew they were likely to face reprisals during this period. But one did not have to be "guilty" of anything, because belonging to the "wrong social class" was often sufficient grounds for harassment, such as denial of promotion or difficulties with university admissions.

Small shopkeepers were harassed, as Bronislaw Pindelski, the owner of a small ice cream store, vividly recounts: "Three tax inspectors all of a sudden waltzed into the shop. One of them, probably the boss, introduced himself and flashed his super-inspection order. 'You will turn out all the customers now,' he ordered. 'There will be a detailed search. We need to examine your swindles. Each small business owner is a thief and wheeler-dealer. There can be no private shops on Obrońców Stalingradu [Stalingrad Defender's] Street. It's a shame for this heroic street.'"[29]

After Stalin's death in 1953 and the new head of state Nikita Khrushchev's reckoning with Stalinism three years later in his famous secret speech at the Twentieth Party Congress of the CPSU, a wave of anti-Stalinism also emerged in Poland. But when protests against the Communists and the Soviet Union broke out in 1956, the situation almost spiraled out of control and there was a risk that the Soviet Union would launch a military intervention, similar to its intervention in Hungary in the same year. The party leader, Edward Ochab, who had only just taken office, was removed and replaced by Wladyslaw Gomulka. The Soviets initially rejected him, which increased his popularity in Poland. Although Poland remained a dictatorship, repression was no longer as severe as it had been during the Stalinist period. Gomulka put the brakes on the collectivization of private agriculture, which his predecessors had not made much progress with, and allowed small private enterprises on a limited scale. Of 10,000 agricultural cooperatives still in existence in September 1956, only 1,500 remained by the end of the year.[30]

This and the end of the campaign against the "kulaks" boosted Gomulka's popularity among the rural population. While by 1960 more than 90 percent of land had been collectivized in the USSR, the GDR, and Bulgaria, more than 80 percent in Czechoslovakia and Romania, and 71 percent in Hungary, only 13 percent of land in Poland was owned by the state.[31] In 1959, food production reached its highest level since the end of World War II, and this was almost entirely due to small- and medium-sized farmers. In the mid-1950s, the number of skilled trade businesses doubled and the number of small stores increased by 80 percent.[32]

However, it became increasingly clear that the planned economy system was not working in Poland either. In 1956 and 1957, economic reforms were discussed. In January 1957, an Economic Council was convened under the leadership of the economist Oskar Lange, who advocated a number of modest economic reforms within the framework of the existing system. Despite the fact that the proposals were moderate and by no means called for a return to capitalism, the party leadership rejected them. There had already been repeated attempts at reform in the socialist country, all of which had one thing in common: the reformers wanted to introduce more competition and market mechanisms to give enterprises greater autonomy in their decision-making. But they shied away from taking the decisive step, namely questioning the dogma of state ownership of the means of production and the planned economy.

Although living standards improved, Poland fell further and further behind in comparison with other countries, as Friszke and Dudek point out: "A comparison of Poland's economic performance with countries that had been at a similar level of development in the 1930s and the 1940s shows that, in the mid-1960s, Poland began to lose the modernization race, both in terms of economic criteria [...] and in terms of standard-of-living indicators. Real wages grew less than 2 percent annually, which meant virtual stagnation. The average citizen spent about 50 percent of their income on food, and about 18 percent on clothing."[33]

In the early 1970s, under a government led by Edward Gierek (1970–1980), the standard of living improved in Poland, and the Polish sociologist Gavin Rae speaks of "a period of remarkable economic growth [...] combined with surges in incomes, consumption and living standards."[34] But this growth was based on ever-increasing foreign debt, which was a cause of later, even greater problems. The socialist economic system proved incapable of generating sustainable growth.

By the end of the 1970s, the economic situation came to a head once again: quarter after quarter, the quantities of goods decreased, and the queues in front of stores, especially butchers' shops, became longer and longer. "In order to purchase more expensive goods, such as refrigerators, televisions, furniture and the like, prospective buyers had to wait in line for several days. Such a drastic shortage of goods gave rise to a widespread system of corruption, and mutual favors within the framework of old-boy networks became commonplace. For example, there was a great advantage in knowing a salesman who could 'put aside' the coveted goods. Since representatives at the various levels of power had access to goods that were in short supply, they had plenty of opportunities to recruit their 'clientele.' The life of an average citizen gradually became more and more difficult, so that in the course of the constant 'hunt' for basic goods and hours spent standing in lines, frustration and aggression increased."[35]

Above all, the problem with getting hold of meat was persistent. One proposed solution, that in some mysterious way was supposed to mitigate the problem, was to introduce so-called "meatless Mondays" in 1959. From that time on, it was forbidden not only to sell but also to consume any meat on Mondays. "Nowadays the Catholics fast on Fridays, and Marxists on Mondays," a journalist commented ironically.[36]

To better understand what everyday life was like in socialist Poland, I traveled to Warsaw, where I met Alicja Wancerz-Gluza, co-founder of the Karta Center, a non-governmental historical archive. Alicja was initially active in the independent trade union *Solidarność*, founded in 1980, and in the anti-communist underground after martial law was declared in Poland in December 1981. On January 4, 1982, together with her husband and a small group of friends, she founded the underground newspaper *Karta*, which opposed the newly installed regime under General Jaruzelski. This later evolved into the Karta Archive, which collected an extensive selection of materials, including 6,000 interviews with contemporary witnesses and approximately 400,000 photos and other documents.

During our conversation, Alicja explained the realities of everyday life in Poland under the socialist planned economy. She showed me the pile of ration cards that Polish people needed to buy food and other products until the collapse of the socialist regime in the late 1980s. The first ration cards were for sugar in 1976. Until the end of socialism, more and more of these ration cards were added for all kinds of products, including meat, fat, butter, detergent, soap, cigarettes, gasoline, and even shoes. There were also special tokens on the ration cards, and these were numbered. For example, it might suddenly be announced that you could buy school supplies for children or sanitary pads for women using token number 3.

The whole ration card system involved an enormous bureaucracy, characteristic of planned economies: Two hundred thousand people worked in the distribution of the ration cards, another 40,000 dealt with their administration, and another 6,000 with inspections. All workplaces, universities, schools, and housing administrations were also burdened with the work of administering the ration cards.[37]

In practice, the ration card system worked as follows: in every shop, the sales people would use scissors to cut the small token from the ration cards. To get a ration card with a special token,

Poles needed another card, which their employers used to register all the cards they had been issued each month. For example, if you went on holiday for a fortnight, you had to hand in your ration cards at the hotel beforehand and be given new cards so that you could eat while you were on holiday. And it was a real tragedy if someone lost one of their ration cards. Joanna Solska writes ironically in her book about life under socialism in Poland in the 1980s: "You lost your ration card? You had to change your diet. You should not lose your ration cards because there were no duplicates. If somebody lost their meat ration card, they would have to become a vegetarian for the rest of the month."[38]

Adds Alicja: "It was a truly special occasion when I got a special card from the registry office that would allow me to buy white tights for my wedding. I was also given a certificate stating that because we were getting married, we were allowed to buy gold wedding rings in a jewelry store. But we didn't have the money for that, and we didn't want rings anyway. So, there were special cards for all occasions, for example, for a funeral you could get a card for black pantyhose." But just because you had a ration card didn't mean you could go out and buy what you wanted. Often you had to stand in line for hours to get what you wanted. People also exchanged their cards if they needed a different product to the one their card allowed. For example, a vodka card (an adult was allowed to buy one bottle per month) could be exchanged for a coffee card.

For children, there were cards for powdered milk and sweets (so-called "chocolate substitutes"). To buy furniture, a washing machine, or a television, people had to stand in what were known as *"kolejki społeczne"* (social lines). In some cases, they had to join the line every day for a month or two, queuing for hours at a time. Family members joined the queue and waited in line and swapped places with other family members every few hours.

Often it was the grandfather or grandmother who was chosen to stand in line because they were the most likely to have the time to persevere in line for many days. Every couple of hours, names were called out, and if someone had left the line, they lost their place and the time they had spent in line didn't count.

Joanna Solska also reports that when something was delivered to a shop, people bought it even if they didn't need it at all, because they could use it in underground barter transactions to exchange for something else: "If you saw a guy carrying two potties, the reason probably wasn't that he was a father of twins. Perhaps he didn't even have any kids at all. For bystanders it was obvious, that there was an option to buy two potties in the shop."[39]

It was also difficult to get a telephone. "In my neighborhood, in 1986, there was only one phone booth for all of the streets and buildings in the new district," explains Alicja. "It was a public phone, no one in my neighborhood had a private phone." Her parents moved into their cooperative apartment in 1960 and immediately applied for a telephone line. The phone was eventually connected thirteen years later, in 1973. And that only happened so "quickly" because her father was a member of the Polish United Workers' Party. Normally you had to wait even longer for a telephone in socialist Poland—on average, 18 years. This was partly due to the weaknesses of the planned economy system, but also had political reasons: "Fewer phones meant fewer conversations to control, and less conspiracy and trouble."[40] In any case, international calls could only be made at the post office, where people had to book a phone call several hours in advance. By 1987, only 12 percent of Poles had a telephone.[41] This compared with around 16 percent of the people in the GDR and 99 percent in West Germany in 1989.[42]

Cars were also few and far between. In Poland, only around 14 percent of the population owned a car in 1990;[43] in West Germany the figure was almost 68 percent.[44] Poles had to wait several years for a car, without the certainty of actually being able to buy one in the end. Of course, it was possible to buy a used car, but they were sometimes even more expensive than a new car. It was only because Alicja's father was in the party that he received a special voucher for a car, a Fiat 126p. But he had to wait until 1980, when he got the voucher as a reward for becoming First Party Secretary in his factory.

People had to wait for everything, including an apartment. Alicja remembers: "When my future husband was five years old, his parents started paying money into a cooperative, so that twenty-five years later they would have the right to buy a small apartment. My parents started saving a little later because they had to save for my older sister first." Twenty-five years later, when she was twenty-nine and her husband thirty, they were able to pool the entitlements they had acquired over many years of saving and move into a small three-room apartment, which was nevertheless far from debt-free and still had to be paid off.

Small shopkeepers were still being harassed in the 1970s, as Mieczyslaw F. Rakowski, editor-in-chief of the weekly *Polityka*, noted in his diary in March 1975: "I had a chance to watch the work of the First Secretary of the Provincial Committee [...]. When we were going along a street, he pointed to a small private shop and said: 'We still have a few small business owners, but we are already doing away with them. There was a small business owner over there, he was selling ice cream. There was always a line in front of his shop. I ordered a back tax of half a million on him. He paid without a murmur. So, I ordered another half a million on him. He could not stand it. And he is gone now.' This is how our nice little secretary is ruling. Goddammit!"[45]

The situation would certainly have been worse and the system would have collapsed sooner if it were not for the emergence of an extensive black market, explains Piotr Korys in his book *Poland from Partitions to EU Accession:* "The grey economy and corruption were the mechanisms making it possible to survive in the planned economy, as they reduced the inefficiency generated by the planner's decisions and introduced the element of the market. Similarly, 'black market' became a kind of 'foundation' that underpinned the official market for consumer goods (which was in the state of persistent disequilibrium). Therefore, even though these practices were indictable, the authorities tolerated them, and even partly controlled them by means of the secret intelligence service."[46]

In her book *Życie w PRL: I strasznie i śmiesznie* (in English, literally *Life in Communist Poland: The Terrifying and The Ridiculous*), Iwona Kienzler illustrates just how important the black market became in Poland: even farmers had to buy tools and machines on the black market because in state-owned shops they were not available. Farmers had serious problems with access to a range of simple products, such as binder twine, which became a symbol of the ineffectiveness of the socialist economy, because its shortages on the market handicapped the work during the crop season in the whole country. And it was the case every year throughout the whole period of socialism. After the year 1989, as if with a touch of a magic wand, the problem disappeared. Today Poland is an exporter of binder twine.[47]

The journalist Piotr Andrzejewski wrote about the black market in 1986: "Krzysio has a 100 percent profit on oranges bought in Hamburg for 1.6 marks. Of course, we may not like Krzysio—he's a money-grubber and an unpleasant man. I must admit, however, that I dislike even more the fact that the bureaucratic machine of our trade cannot solve the problem of supplying our market with citrus fruits. And when that behemoth announces with a fanfare that it will flood the Polish market with citrus fruits, and then lets half of the fruits decay before reaching the shops, I keep asking where the worker-peasant inspection is? Who should it deal with in the first place: Krzysio, or the guy responsible for the lemon scandal?"[48]

On the subject of oranges, there is another story that comes to mind: a Polish blogger explains why holidays in communist Poland always made her think of oranges: "So you might ask, why would holidays in communist Poland remind me of oranges? Well, the holidays were the only time that people got citrus fruits under communism. It was such a big deal that regular updates on national TV would track the locations of the ships carrying different citrus fruits to our shores."[49] Marcin Zielinski tells me that even today, his grandmother still gives him oranges for Christmas because, after her experiences during the socialist era, she considers them to be something particularly desirable and rare.

The communists in Poland cannot be accused of not having repeatedly tried to reform the system. But since the reforms remained within the confines of the system, i.e., they shied away from questioning the inherent features of socialist economics, they were doomed to failure. As Bartlomiej Kaminski demonstrates in his book *The Collapse of State Socialism*, the reforms in the 1980s actually increased the problems of the economy in some cases. At first glance, the reforms adopted in 1981 seemed very radical and far-reaching, even more so than the reforms in Hungary and Yugoslavia.[50] The magic formula was SSS: self-dependent, self-managed, and self-financed. Self-managed meant that decisions would be shifted to the factory level to be made by workers. Self-financed meant that companies would receive less support from the state and that a closer link would be established between their economic performance and the remuneration of workers and management. Self-dependent stood for greater independence from central government planning authorities.[51]

One of the key features of the reforms in the 1980s was that, in some cases, financial incentives replaced government commands. "The introduced reform measures changed the mix of public policy tools in favor of the financial instruments, which are theoretically tools of indirect controls. The problem was that they could be used only as tools of direct controls because the reform measures introduced fell well short of decoupling the state from the economy."[52]

The reforms were intended to improve socialism, not to abolish it. State ownership of the means of production, the essential feature of socialism, remained largely untouched. There was a reluctance to introduce a true market economy and, in the end, there were even more regulations and inconsistencies to become entangled in, making the situation worse, not better. "The conclusion that can be drawn from the analysis of the Polish experiment with economic reform is that use of market measures in a nonmarket environment brings about the worst of worlds. The 'monetization' of central controls produced galloping inflation coexisting with shortages. The absence of competition and markets produced pressures toward increasing the scope of direct microeconomic intervention by the state."[53]

The many attempts at reform[54] nevertheless achieved something good: they destroyed any illusions of a "third way" between capitalism and socialism. Gavin Rae is right when he writes that it is inconceivable that the original *Solidarność* movement would have approved of a reform program as radical as the one implemented from 1990 onward, and that this did not correspond to what had been agreed upon at the so-called "Round Table" talks between the communist regime and the trade union the year before.[55] But Rae is also correct in stating: "The failure of successive reforms, in the latter years of the socialist period, helped to strengthen the belief in society that the system was unreformable and that there needed to be a clean political and economic break from the past."[56] This gave a chance to a real reformer, Leszek Balcerowicz. He understood that reforms within the framework of the existing system would be futile and that only overcoming socialism and introducing capitalism could lead to improvement; but, more on this later.

The record of the socialist economy was sobering. In 1989, Poland was one of the poorest countries in Europe. The average Pole earned less than $50 a month, which wasn't even equivalent in value to one-tenth of what people in the Federal Republic of Germany (West Germany) were earning. Even taking into account differences in purchasing power, in 1989 a Pole earned less than one-third as much as a West German.[57] And Marcin Zielinski explains, the term purchasing power had a very different meaning in a socialist country like Poland than in capitalist economies. In Poland, the figure on the price tag might have been low, but it was hard to get the product.

"Poles were poorer than an average citizen of Gabon, Ukraine, or Suriname. Poland's income lagged behind even its communist peers: its GDP per capita amounted to only half of the level of income in Czechoslovakia," writes Piatkowski. [58]

During the years 1988 and 1989, the shelves in many Polish stores were even emptier than the shelves in other communist countries. Stores often stocked just bread, milk, and vinegar. And even the most basic foodstuffs could only be obtained in exchange for coupons.[59] The infrastructure was also run down. Across the country, there were less than 200 kilometers of mostly old, German-built highways.[60] Conditions were so miserable and no one expected Poland to become the stage for an economic miracle over the next few decades. Experts would have expected Hungary to lead the way, or perhaps Czechoslovakia, the GDR (East Germany), or Slovenia. But Poland? No one was predicting a Polish success story given the poor situation from which it started.[61]

Political Transformation

The conditions for Poland's economic miracle were created by the political transformation of Poland that began in the 1980s. The decisive impetus for the end of the socialist dictatorship came from the workers. Poland's entire post-war history is punctuated by repeated strikes and ongoing protests by the country's workers, many of which were brutally suppressed. For example, there were the strikes that started in the Gdansk shipyard on December 14, 1970. On the night of December 15, the striking workers were surrounded by army units with tanks. When the workers left the plant, the soldiers opened fire on them before marching onto the premises. That same day, strikes also broke out at the Gdynia shipyard. There were fatalities and injuries. Friszke and Dudek relate the night's events as follows: "The brutality of the soldiers sent to repress the strikes—not only during the events in the streets, but also toward those already detained—was shocking. In prisons and temporary detention centers, people were beaten unconscious and seriously injured."[62] I visited the Gdansk shipyard, which is now home to two museums and a memorial plaque in January 2023. The memorial plaque lists the names of the workers who were killed at that time, the youngest of whom were fifteen, sixteen, and seventeen years old.

Strikes and demonstrations also occurred in many other cities during that week of December 1970, and resulted in the loss of forty-five lives. Of the victims, twelve were under the age of twenty and twenty-four were under the age of thirty. In total, 1,100 people were wounded, the majority of whom were workers.[63] Of great psychological importance was the fact that, in October 1978, a Pole, Karol Józef Wojtyła, born in Wadowice in 1920, was elected Pope John Paul II. Poles greeted the news with unbridled enthusiasm, and the new pope clearly stood for the values of freedom. Millions of Poles lined the streets to greet him when he visited his homeland in June 1979.

August 1980 marked the start of a new wave of strikes. Workers at the Lenin Shipyard in Gdansk demanded not only higher wages but also official recognition for a free-trade union. It is remarkable that the working class, which was supposedly the ruling class in the "dictatorship of the proletariat," was the force that repeatedly rebelled against the country's rulers and lent weight to their discontent with strikes and demonstrations. The communist government was finally forced to cave in to the workers' demands and officially recognize the union. Soon, around ten million Poles joined *Solidarność*. At the same time, party members increasingly deserted the PZPR communist party. By 1981, 350,000 members had left the PZPR, overwhelmingly workers.[64]

The Soviet Union was rightly afraid of this development as it threatened to send a strong signal to other socialist states. In Poland, people were afraid that the Soviet Union might launch a military intervention, as it had done in East Berlin in 1953, Budapest in 1956, and Prague in 1968. On December 13, 1981, the government imposed martial law in Poland and imprisoned the popular workers' leader, Lech Walesa. *Solidarność* and the entire opposition were forced underground.

The economic situation continued to deteriorate and, in the late 1980s, the country was engulfed by a new wave of general strikes. The Polish government had little choice but to agree to the "Round Table" talks, which started in February 1989. These talks involved not only the PZPR communist party, but also the *Solidarność* trade union and the Catholic Church, which was then even more powerful and influential in Poland than it is today. One result of the Round Table talks was the legalization of *Solidarność*; another was to hold elections that, while not up to the standard of free elections in democratic countries, were quite different from the typical sham elections held in communist states. Free elections were held for 161 of the 460 seats in the Polish parliament, the *Sejm*. In previous elections, the candidates had all come from either the PZPR or other parties loyal to the regime; now, for the first time, independent candidates were allowed to stand. In addition, the talks secured the reintroduction of a second chamber of parliament, the Senate. Here, an entirely free election to the 100-seat Senate was assured. The *Sejm* election of June 4, 1989, saw the *Solidarność* Civic Committee achieve an absolute majority of the freely contested seats in the first round of voting. After the second round of voting, it was clear that in addition to the 161 *Solidarność Sejm* deputies, ninety-nine of the party's 100 candidates for the Senate had also won.

Balcerowicz and His Economic Reforms

Meanwhile, the economic situation in socialist Poland seemed hopeless. Even sections within the ruling party had by now realized that the only thing that could possibly save Poland was increased entrepreneurial freedom. Therefore, on September 27, 1988, the entrepreneur Mieczysław Wilczek, who had been an advisor to various committees of the *Sejm* since 1985, was appointed Minister of Industry (*Minister przemysłu*) by Prime Minister Mieczysław Rakowski. Wilczek held his ministerial post until the end of Rakowski's term, when he was replaced by Tadeusz Syryjczyk on September 12, 1989. In 1988, Wilczek presented a bill on business activity (*ustawa o działalności gospodarczej*), also known as *Wilczek's Act (Ustawa Wilczka)*, which initiated the establishment of small businesses in the final months of the Polish People's Republic. In simple terms, the law allowed every Polish citizen to engage in any economic activity they wanted.

That the ruling communists accepted such a law was an act of desperation that has been compared to Lenin's New Economic Policy (NEP).[65] In the early 1920s, even the leader of the Soviet October Revolution was forced to recognize that a continuation of the communists' radical economic policy would have threatened the very foundations of Soviet power. Industrial production had already fallen to one-tenth of its 1913 level, and people were starving. In response, Lenin initiated a U-turn and proposed a New Economic Policy, which was adopted at the Tenth Congress of the Russian Communist Party in March 1921. Lenin conceded that "we have sustained a very severe defeat on the economic front."[66] Lenin was clever enough to realize that the only available solution was "reverting to capitalism to a considerable extent—to what extent we do not know."[67] These are the very words used by Lenin to formulate his policy shift.

The Soviet Union's NEP legalized profit-oriented production, private ownership in the production of consumer goods, and the acquisition of wealth. It also integrated peasants into the economic system through the introduction of a "natural tax." Lenin allowed state-owned enterprises to lease their factories to private individuals and place matters of finance, logistics, and entrepreneurship in private hands. In July 1921, freedom of trade was even restored for craftspeople and small industrial enterprises.[68]

Wilczek's Act in Poland went even further. It included, for example:

> Article 1: Taking up and conducting business activity is free and allowed for everyone on equal rights, while complying with the conditions set out by the legal regulations.

Article 2: An entity carrying out business, hereinafter referred to as the 'business entity,' may be an individual, legal person, or organizational unit without legal personality, established in accordance with the legal provisions.

Article 4: Business entities may, as part of their business activity, perform acts and actions which are not prohibited by law.

Article 5: A business entity may employ an unlimited number of employees without the agency of employment authorities.[69]

Many Poles must have regarded the new law as the ultimate Christmas present, especially as it was passed on December 23, 1988. Entrepreneur Roman Kluska, founder of Optimus, remembers how wonderfully easy it suddenly was to set up a new business: "To learn how to run a company at that time, it was enough to read a few acts: the Commercial Code, Tax Law, Customs Law, and Labor Code. I did it overnight. There were tens of thousands of people like me in Poland at that time. Each of them set up a small business and got down to work. Work and mental prowess were the only things that counted. Those were beautiful times. No clerk had a lot to say. And the tax law was so simple that, when there was an inspection, I did not even have to offer a cup of tea to the inspector."[70]

The result was impressive and the law unleashed a wave of entrepreneurial initiative. Poles had been waiting for economic freedom for so long, and now it finally seemed to have arrived. Sebastian Stodolak, vice president of the Warsaw Enterprise Institute, explains: "The entrepreneurship of Poles, suppressed for years, was finally released. Poles put up stalls, mobile foldable tin stalls, and started to trade. They took out their cash 'stashed under their pillows' and started to set up businesses. Some two million firms were set up and six million jobs were created in the period of a dozen or so months."[71]

Until then, private business activity often took place under absurd conditions. Alicja from the Karta Archive recalls: "In mid-1988, a friend offered me a job in a newly established computer company that wanted to help people who came from the underground, persecuted former prisoners, and so on. The company imported computers from Singapore and Hong Kong. It was a very difficult process because computers could only be bought by private individuals 'for personal use.' The risk was high and you had to wait many weeks for a package that you could never be sure would actually arrive. But if you got a computer, you could later 'give it' to someone else. For example, an aunt would give the computer to her nephew, and only he in turn could sell the computer through our company [...]. It was crazy and you had to be very creative to get around the nonsensical regulations. But the profit from selling a computer was enormous! My husband and I also bought a computer thanks to the help of an 'experienced' friend and borrowed money."

Mieczyslaw Wilczek's reforms were the last of many attempts to implement change within the framework of the socialist system; an attempt that already pointed beyond the system itself. On the one hand, the reforms had a positive impact, but on the other, there were also negative aspects, as Marcin Zielinski observes: "As a partial solution, it could lead to oligarchization of the economy as it allowed *nomenklatura* (high-ranking officials) to reap economic benefits from their social position. For example, many private companies were established by *nomenklatura* members who directed state-owned enterprises with which they cooperated as the business's owners. The incentive was to make profits with private companies and losses with SOEs and eventually to lead them to bankruptcy to make the takeover possible."

As mentioned, more and more people in Poland were realizing that the planned economy was not working. A number of economists had even started to think about how to overcome the system. One of them was Leszek Balcerowicz, who would later play a major role in turning the Polish economy around. Balcerowicz was born in Lipno in 1947 and studied foreign trade at the Central School of Planning and Statistics in Warsaw, "probably the most open economic faculty in the socialist countries."[72] He was awarded his doctorate in 1975. His doctoral dissertation was based on an extensive study of the Western literature on technical change. In the late 1960s, he joined the Polish United Workers' Party (PZPR) because he thought that the only way to bring about change was from within the party. At the time, almost no one believed that the one-party socialist system would ever come to an end, let alone a peaceful one.

Balcerowicz was awarded a scholarship to the United States in the 1970s, where he completed his studies with a Master of Business Administration, an exceptional achievement for a Pole under the political conditions of the time. As *Solidarność* was being formed, he founded a team to draw up plans for economic reform. Like the other reformers, he began with ideas that would lead to more market economy and competition within the framework of a socialist system, but he soon realized that no real changes were possible within the narrow corset of a planned economy. "I was struck by the *naiveté* of the 'socialist side' represented by Oskar Lange et al., and the reasonableness of the 'antisocialist' camp, represented by Ludwig von Mises and Friedrich August von Hayek. I fully shared von Mises's ironic prediction that the effective reform of socialism entails a return to capitalism."[73]

Balcerowicz studied economic success stories such as those of Taiwan, South Korea, and Ludwig Erhard's economic reforms in Germany, and juxtaposed them with the futile attempts to implement reforms within socialist systems. In the spring of 1989, he wrote a paper on the need for reforms in Poland, in which he argued for rapid liberalizations. At that time, he had no idea that a few months later he would be responsible for reforming the Polish economy. He had never even planned to enter politics.

But the June 1989 elections, which ended with a landslide victory for *Solidarność*, changed everything including his own life. At the end of August 1989, the new Polish Prime Minister Tadeusz Mazowiecki asked Balcerowicz to become his Ludwig Erhard (Ludwig Erhard had introduced the market economy in West Germany after the Second World War). From 1989 to 1991, Balcerowicz served as Deputy Prime Minister and Minister of Finance in the first non-communist governments under Mazowiecki and his successor Jan Krzysztof Bielecki.

Poland's initial macroeconomic conditions were particularly difficult; more so than in many other socialist countries. In addition to the general problems from which all socialist planned economies suffered, Poland was gripped by rampant inflation and a mountain of debt. Its debt burden to Western creditors had grown larger and larger and, by 1984, Poland was the third-largest debtor in the world.[74] Poland's gross foreign debt (mainly to capitalist countries) ballooned from $1.1 billion in 1971 to $40 billion in 1989, more than in any other socialist country.[75] In 1989, annualized inflation was 640 percent in Poland, compared to 18.9 percent in Hungary, 10 percent in Bulgaria, and as low as 1.5 and 0.6 percent in Czechoslovakia and Romania, respectively.[76]

Another initial condition that may, at first glance, seem positive actually had a very negative side. As previously mentioned, and in contrast to other socialist countries, attempts at large-scale collectivization of agriculture in Poland were aborted when peasant resistance proved too strong: "However, the average size of the 2.7 million private farms was only 7.2 hectares, and 30 percent of farms had less than two hectares."[77] By comparison, in the Federal Republic of Germany (West Germany), the area cultivated by a single farmer had grown from 2.9 to 12.5 hectares between 1950 and 1989. The extreme fragmentation of farmland was one of the negative initial conditions in Poland.

These were all simply factors specific to Poland that made the situation in the country particularly difficult. More important, of course, were the same problems that every planned-economy system entails: the absence of real prices because prices were set by the state, the absence of competition, a focus not on profit but on production targets set by 'the plan.' All these are the factors that Ludwig von Mises had already identified as early as 1922 in his book *Socialism: An Economic and Sociological Analysis* as the reasons why socialism could not work.

Probably Balcerowicz's key insight, and the reason for the success of his reform program, was that a progressive series of minor reforms would not solve any of these problems. The only way to change the situation was through rapid, comprehensive, and radical reforms in all sectors of the economy. Somewhat unusually for an economist, Balcerowicz also had a good political intuition, and that told him: there is only a very short window of opportunity for reforms in such a troubled situation. Either you use this window of opportunity to implement decisive, rapid reform measures, or you hesitate, and it becomes difficult or even impossible to implement the necessary steps. "The main reason for the success of the Polish economic reforms," explained Balcerowicz, "seems to be the great speed of its early phase, when fundamentals of a liberal economic system and macroeconomic stability were established. It was easier for the supporters of the market-oriented reforms to defend them as a *fait accompli* than it would have been to build reforms gradually in the face of a strong populist opposition in Parliament after the elections of October 1991."[78]

What was Balcerowicz's strategy and how did he implement it? In the short term, it was a matter of containing inflation by introducing a sustainable monetary policy. In addition, the problem of foreign debt had to be addressed through negotiations with creditors. However, the creditors could only be convinced to agree to a debt reduction if they saw that Poland would implement market-economy reforms. That was what Balcerowicz intended to do anyway, but now he had an additional argument for doing so by pointing to the country's foreign creditors. At the same time, he hoped that radical liberalization of prices would improve the supply of goods in the short term, and that this would allow people to notice how the reforms were improving their everyday lives.

Balcerowicz also set himself the task of creating the institutions that play a key role in the functioning of a capitalist economy, such as an independent central bank and a stock exchange. In addition, his reform program called for the privatization of state-owned enterprises and the introduction of import and export controls. The minister elaborated his plan, which was soon christened the Balcerowicz Plan. It was adopted by the government between the end of 1989 and February 1990, and then approved by the Polish parliament in July 1990. Other reforms followed, including a law on insurance, a bankruptcy law, and a tax reform.

The reforms were a great success. Inflation decreased significantly: the annualized consumer price index during the last five months of 1989 stood at about 3,000 percent. CPI inflation (end year) in 1990 was 249 percent, in 1991, 60.4 percent; in 1992, 44.3 percent; and in 1993, 37.6 percent.[79] As can be seen, inflation was greatly reduced, although it was still high. Balcerowicz had the following to say about these numbers: "While the level of inflation is clearly still too high, one should compare Poland's disinflation with those in high-inflation Latin American countries. In Chile and Mexico, it took roughly seven years to reduce three-digit inflation to between 15–20 percent. It should be stressed that disinflation in Poland happened while relative prices were radically altered and that this required huge rises in some key prices, especially those of energy."[80]

One important outcome of Balcerowicz's economic reforms was that Poland was flooded with more and better products. Even Gavin Rae, who is critical of many aspects of the country's transformation (he speaks, for example, of "selling off national companies to foreign capital"), concedes some of the benefits: "shops filled with goods, usually of a far superior quality to those commonly available during socialism. The economy of shortage was destroyed and steadily the availability of high-quality products reached the level of that in the West."[81] This had a major impact on people's everyday lives. And this was especially important because radical reforms always lead to some short-term negative impacts, which will test people's patience. It was therefore all the more important that the majority of Poles also experienced early positive impacts of the reforms.

A predictable negative consequence of economic reforms in all former socialist states was that GDP slumped for a few years before returning to growth. In Poland, the decline was 11.6 percent in 1990 and 7.6 percent in 1991. However, Poland's GDP then rose by 1.5 percent in 1992 and by 4 percent in 1993.[82] Gavin Rae, a critic of "economic shock therapy" in general, has no choice but to admit in his book *Poland's Return to Capitalism*: "Despite its severity, the fall in GDP was relatively mild in relation to many other countries in CEE [Central and Eastern Europe]. Another feature of the Polish transition was that growth returned quicker than any other CEE economy."[83]

When interpreting these data, it is important to remember that the levels of GDP under socialism were largely inflated due to wasteful investment and massive military expenditure. In fact, Poland's economic performance was better than the official statistics, which, for example, did not capture the rapid growth of the private sector (of which a significant proportion could be attributed to the unofficial "gray" economy).[84]

The same is also true of unemployment rates, which rose from zero to 12 percent in 1991 and then again to 14 percent in 1992, before remaining at that level for the next few years.[85] In no socialist country were official figures allowed to paint a negative picture: there could be no unemployment, poverty, serious crime, or environmental degradation. People were statistically counted as employed even if they were not engaged in any truly meaningful economic activity. With regard to the GDR (East Germany), for example, the Institute for Economic Research (ifo) calculated that 15 percent of the population, i.e., 1.4 million people, were in reality without work, even if this looked different on paper[86] and everyone technically had a job in some combine, factory, shop, government office, or even a ministry or other institution. Experts refer to this as hidden unemployment. In Poland, the extent of this hidden unemployment was even greater. Estimates showed that in the 1980s, hidden unemployment involved a significant proportion of the workforce. The highest unemployment was recorded in 1981 and 1982. In the general economy, it amounted to approximately 29 percent, and in Polish industry as much as 38 percent. In other years, it oscillated between 20 and 25 percent in the general economy and between 30 and 35 percent in industry.[87]

Exact figures are difficult to estimate, but hidden unemployment may have been as high as 20 to 30 percent.[88] The communists were very creative in the methods they employed to hide unemployment; one paper details how manipulated depictions and statistics were used to hide about six million unemployed.[89]

Iwona Kienzler reports in her book on everyday life in communist Poland, *Życie w PRL. I strasznie i śmiesznie*:

> The state was the main employer. It had the monopoly on labor, but it also had a duty to provide a job for every citizen. What's more, a job for everybody was guaranteed by the constitution of 1952, which obligated the state to provide jobs and wages to everybody. In effect a paradox emerged—the main point of work was … coming to work. Plants and factories produced mainly jobs, as goods made in them often had absolutely no use. The whole situation was perfectly captured by a popular joke:
>
> – Mr. Supervisor, me and Jozef decided to stop drinking and smoking during work.
> – Ok, great. But what will you do then?[90]

Even the communist leaders told each other jokes about the country's supposedly non-existent unemployment. In April 1987, General Jaruzelski met Soviet President Gorbachev and told him that Poland's problems were partly caused by the fiction of full employment. He illustrated this with a joke: "Two guys are pushing the same wheelbarrow. Someone asks them: 'Why are two of you doing that?' They reply: 'Because the third guy is on sick leave.'"[91]

After the end of socialism, hidden unemployment became official unemployment. It was inevitable that people who worked in state-owned enterprises, which were nowhere near competitive enough for global markets and had not been allowed to go bankrupt thanks to state subsidies, would now lose their jobs and that their hidden unemployment would be added to the official unemployment figures. The state-owned enterprises shrank. But at the same time numerous new enterprises were created. Between

1990 and 1993, Leszek Balcerowicz reports, more than one million new private firms were established in Poland.[92] Privatization of the large state-owned enterprises did not proceed as quickly, but many of these firms, Balcerowicz explains, "underwent a radical down-sizing by selling or leasing assets to the private sector, which contributed to the development of that private sector."[93] This led to enormous growth in private sector employment. The share of the private sector, excluding agriculture and cooperatives, grew from 13.2 percent of the total workforce in 1989 to 34.4 percent in 1992, finds Balcerowicz: "If we include agriculture and cooperatives, the share of employment in the private sector jumps to about 60 percent of employment at the end of 1992 and to about 50 percent of GDP."[94]

Ordinary people who had previously worked as employees or civil servants set up their own businesses or became self-employed. In a letter to the magazine *Kobieta I Zycie*, Jaroslaw B. wrote: "I was an average ordinary clerk in one of the central institutions in Poland's capital. I was sitting behind a desk, putting papers from the right to the left, participating in long conferences which achieved nothing, from time to time I got a small pay rise, which made me extremely proud, and—as a man over forty—I started to long for a pension. When the decision to disband my office was made, I was sure it was the end of the world [...]. By coincidence, I bumped into an old friend of mine from the technical college on the Number 15 tram in Warsaw. Witus was dressed in the latest fashion and started the conversation by complaining that he had just left his Volvo in the garage and had been forced to squeeze onto such a crowded streetcar. Naturally, I showed interest in how my former mate was making a living. And he was making his living from his knowledge. He reminded me that we were economist technicians and that I also graduated from a sociological college [...]. I started very slowly, cautiously, with my heart in my mouth, but somehow, step by step, everything developed as I hoped. I took my economy books out from under my bed, hired two bookkeepers from my former central state office, and it turned out that working for myself was simply fascinating."[95]

Many people were swept away by the new spirit of capitalism and wanted to earn money, including children. Maciej Duszyński wrote in a letter to *Cash* magazine in 1993: "My name is Maciej Duszyński and I am ten years old. My Dad reads *Cash* and that is how I came across it. I wish there were a magazine like this for kids, to teach us economics and capitalism and tell us how to make money honestly."[96]

The growth of the private sector led to a decline in the economy's unhealthy concentration on large state-owned enterprises. The number of employees in industrial firms with between fifty-one and 100 employees increased by 202 percent between 1989 and 1991, while the number of employees working in firms with more than 5,000 employees declined by 35.6 percent.[97]

Poland also suddenly became attractive for foreign investors. In 1989, foreign companies invested a meager $60 million in Poland; by 1993, this figure had risen to $1.5 billion.[98] Gavin Rae decries this as a sell-out to foreigners, but this is absurd as foreign investments were only very rarely connected with privatizations. More than 80 percent of foreign investments in the 1990s had nothing to do with privatizations at all. In fact, foreign investments were an important aspect of Poland's integration into the global economy, which had a very rapid and positive impact on the everyday lives of Poles. For example, in blue- and white-collar households, stereo radio ownership increased from 22.6 to 40.8 percent between 1989 and 1992, and ownership of color television sets shot up from 50.7 to 91.4 percent. In 1989, less than 5 percent of these households owned a video cassette recorder (VCR); by 1992, more than half did. The proportion of blue- and white-collar workers who had a washing machine, a freezer, or a car also increased by at least 10 percentage points in each case from 1989 to 1992.

The increase among pensioner households was even greater: in 1989, only 5.4 percent of retirees owned a stereo radio; by 1992, this figure had risen to 13.4 percent. The proportion who owned a VCR rose from 0.7 to 13.5 percent. And while only 30.4 percent of farmers owned their own car in 1989, by 1992 the figure was 41.7 percent. Among retiree households, the percentage who owned a car rose from 9.2 to 15 percent in that short time.[99]

Even more remarkable than the short-term successes were the long-term effects of Poland's economic reforms. In 2017, the economist Marcin Piatkowski published a book, *Europe's Growth Champion*, in which he takes stock after twenty-five years: "Yet, twenty-five years later it is Poland that has become the unrivalled leader of transition and Europe's and the world's growth champion. Since the beginning of post-communist transition in 1989, Poland's economy has grown more than in any other country of Europe. Poland's GDP per capita increased almost two-and-a-half times, beating all other post-communist states as well as the euro-zone."[100]

According to data from the World Bank, GDP per capita in 1989 was 30.1 percent of the corresponding figure in the US and had risen to 48.4 percent of the US level by 2016.[101] Such gains made themselves felt in people's lives. The income of Poles grew from about $10,300 in 1990, adjusted for purchasing power, to almost $27,000 in 2017.[102]

In comparison with the EU-15, the income of Poles was less than one-third in 1989 and had risen to almost two-thirds in 2015. Although East Germany received billions in subsidies from West Germany, the income of Poles, in relative terms, improved more than that of East Germans.[103] Poland's growth was also remarkable in global terms—the country's economy managed to grow faster than the high-growth Asian countries of South Korea, Singapore, and Malaysia.[104] Based on World Bank data, Marcin Piatkowski calculates that "Poland is close to beating the world in the persistence of economic growth. It has grown without interruption from 1992 until 2017, twenty-five years in a row, beating the historical records of South Korea, Singapore, and Japan."[105] Then, unfortunately, the Covid crisis came along and led to a slump, as it did in almost all countries.

Anti-capitalists complain that the rich benefit more from economic growth than the poor. If we compare the incomes of Poles in 1989 and 2016, we can indeed see that the incomes of the richest 10 percent of Poles increased by 135 percent, while average incomes grew by "just" 100 percent and those of the poorest 10 percent of the population by 40 percent.[106] Anyone who is primarily interested in the issue of inequality will criticize such developments, while anyone who is primarily interested in the issue of eradicating poverty will note that, most importantly, all sections of the population benefited.

More importantly, the poor of twenty years ago are by no means the exact same people who are poor today. When it comes to poverty, analyses often wrongly assume that the income and population categories always refer to the same real-world people. This entirely overlooks what is most important, namely the question of what opportunities for advancement a person enjoys. And social mobility in Poland is very high. "A series of large sociological surveys on more than 30,000 respondents conducted during 2011–2015 found that more than 40 percent of households from the bottom 20 percent of households moved to higher group levels, while 40 percent of households in the top 20 percent moved down to lower income levels."[107] Whereby moving down to a lower income level does not necessarily have to be synonymous with a decrease in absolute income. So, anyone who is classed as poor in relative terms by no means has to remain poor, and the reverse is also true, of course: the rich have no guarantee of remaining rich. That is the essence of a true market economy, and it was equally true of Poland.

It is not only the standard of living that has improved dramatically, so has the environmental situation. Anti-capitalists blame private capitalist companies' pursuit of profit for environmental destruction. In fact, however, environmental destruction was much worse in socialist countries. Levels of water and air pollution in Poland decreased rapidly after the end of socialism. This was not primarily a result of the decline in GDP, because the decline in air and water pollution was many times higher. "The amount of waste water fed into rivers in 1992 was 40 percent lower than in 1989; that of liquid pollutants declined by 50 percent, and the emission of gaseous pollutants decreased by 40 percent."[108]

Air quality has also improved significantly. From 1990 to 2019, the number of deaths in Poland attributable to air pollution in a given year decreased significantly, from a peak of 51,800 to 31,100 people.[109] As Piatkowski points out: "In 1980, the amount of energy needed to produce one unit of output and the corresponding pollution was almost eight times higher in CEE than in Western Europe. In Poland's industrialized region of Silesia, the concentration of benzopyrene in the air was ten times higher than in the West, leading to respiratory diseases and premature death. The transition saved the environment. Energy intensity, a ratio of energy consumption to GDP, in Poland and among its regional peers declined at a globally unprecedented pace, from 12,910 Btu per dollar in 1990 to just 6,000 Btu in 2011, only 20 per cent higher than in Germany."[110]

The development in Poland is the same as in other developed capitalist countries: growth decoupled from CO2 emissions, which is quite crucial for the issue of climate change. CO2 emissions rose sharply in the 1960s and 1970s. "Despite a minor fall due to various economic failures, the level still exceeded 11 metric tons per capita in the late 1980s. The transformation changed this picture significantly and in less than ten years the emissions reached around 8 metric tons per capita. Also, there is a growing efficiency of business, as less and less kilograms of CO_2 were emitted per steadily growing GDP."[111] Even today, despite the Polish economy's strong growth, emissions have held steady at around eight metric tons per capita.[112]

Above all, Poles are much happier today. In 2015, 80 percent of Poles were satisfied with their lives, compared with just 50 percent at the beginning of the capitalist transition in 1992.[113] Life expectancy, which was 70.7 years at birth in Poland in 1990, had increased to 78.5 years by 2020.[114]

What Can We Learn from Developments in Poland?

What can other countries learn from Poland? First, it is important to have someone at the head of the reform process who has a clear, market-economy coordinate system. This was the case in Germany after World War II with Ludwig Erhard, and it was the case in the 1980s when Margaret "Maggie" Thatcher in Great Britain and Ronald Reagan in the United States led their countries out of crisis and onto the road to success. In Poland, it was Leszek Balcerowicz who made a decisive contribution to the country's economic success. Like Thatcher, Balcerowicz was an admirer of Hayek. And although Marcin Piatkowski, the author of *Europe's Growth Champion* who is frequently quoted here, is certainly not a disciple of Hayek, he admits that if it were not for Leszek Balcerowicz, the Polish miracle would never have happened.[115]

Perhaps the most crucial factor in the success of the reforms, however, was that Balcerowicz understood that they must be implemented at great speed because there was only a very small window of opportunity before the media and political opponents would deploy populist slogans to stir up public opinion against the reforms. Balcerowicz had come to the conclusion: "Based on my previous studies of reforms and my realization of how dramatic the economic situation in Poland was in 1989, I was deeply convinced that only a radical strategy could succeed, even though risky, because Poland in 1989 was in largely uncharted waters. It was clear to me that a risky strategy was preferable to a hopeless one. It was this reasoned assumption and not an emotional radicalism that gave me the psychological strength to push and persist with radical reforms."[116]

The term "shock therapy" was widely adopted, and I will use it too, although Balcerowicz points out that the word is loaded with inherently negative connotations: "The very expression 'shock therapy' frightens ordinary people, and indeed, it has often been used for that purpose."[117] The reforms, according to Piatkowski, "were implemented at an unprecedented speed." Many were introduced in a "big bang fashion" on January 1, 1990, just four months after the first post-communist government had been formed. "The reform program was among the most radical economic reform programs ever implemented in peace-time in global history."[118]

There were several reasons why action had to be taken so quickly. The first was the dramatic nature of the situation: this was a country on the verge of hyperinflation, goods were in short supply everywhere, and everyone could see that something had to be done quickly. But the rapid reforms were also important for a psychological reason: "Everyone needed to know that communism was gone forever and adjust accordingly."[119] Because, of course, there were old elites who opposed the reforms, and it was important to dash their hopes of a return to socialism. The correctness of the "shock therapy" agenda was confirmed by the fact that Poland was the first post-socialist country that, after a brief recession, returned to growth as early as 1992. Comparative studies of reforms in other post-communist countries proved that "the faster the speed of reforms, the quicker the recovery, and the higher the growth."[120]

An analysis published in 2016, "Twenty-Five Years of Reform in Ex-Communist Countries," clearly refutes the thesis of advocates of gradual reforms ("gradualists") such as Joseph Stiglitz, who argue against rapid and radical reforms: "A key argument for gradualism was that too-rapid reforms would cause great social pain. In reality, rapid reformers experienced shorter recessions and recovered much earlier than gradual reformers."[121] GDP per capita grew faster in countries such as Poland, which implemented radical reforms, than in other former socialist countries. In addition, they attracted much higher levels of foreign investment.[122] The long-term analysis proves that you can pick the winner in the earliest stages of the race: "the basic pattern—of who led the reform process and who lagged behind—was set within the first four to five years."[123]

In all former socialist countries, reforms made the situation worse in the first few years and led to recession and an increase in poverty. Previously hidden unemployment and the misallocation of resources were laid bare for all to see. But countries that implemented early and radical reforms, such as Poland, were the quickest to emerge from this difficult phase, and poverty declined much faster after this lean period than in countries that implemented less radical reforms.[124] Even twenty-five years later, it was still evident that countries such as Poland that implemented radical reforms quickly were in a significantly better position than countries that implemented less radical reforms.[125] Of course, Balcerowicz argues, most successful economic reforms inevitably lead to dissatisfaction, "but little or no reform must sooner or later generate even greater disillusionment and frustration." This is also due to the fact that many people blame the reforms for grievances and social problems that are in fact the result of reforms not going far enough.[126]

Balcerowicz's strength was that he not only was a good economist, but also understood the mechanisms of politics and public opinion. The end of socialism in Poland meant that the country suddenly had a free press. This was a huge step forward, but it also resulted in complicating the reform process: the homogeneous press under socialism hid problems and painted a better, milder picture of the situation. A free press, on the other hand, often focused on describing grievances and problems, true to the old adage: "The only good news is bad news." It was therefore to be expected that the media in Poland would very quickly turn its attention to problems that were, rightly or wrongly, attributed to the reforms.[127] This coverage would also have a decisive influence on the behavior of voters.

Elections were held in Poland on October 27, 1991. This was not ideal; it would have been better for the reformers if they had had another four years until the next election, because by then Poland had returned to growth and the positive results of the reforms were being felt by more of the population. In contrast, 1991 was a difficult year, the second year of recession with declining GDP. Sixty parties contested the election (and twenty-eight of them made it into parliament). Most of these parties adopted a critical position toward the Balcerowicz group's economic reforms.[128] Polish media outlets were full of negative news and demanded a departure from the current course, arguing that the capitalist reforms were making things worse rather than better. "In Poland, especially in 1991, the media bombarded the Polish public with messages that the Polish economy had been struck by economic catastrophe and that there should be a radically new program to improve the situation quickly. The proposed program had three familiar elements: relaxation of monetary and fiscal policies, protectionism, and state intervention at the industry level."[129]

Many problems that had been covered up during the socialist period, such as hidden unemployment, now came to light. The populist slogans blaming capitalist reforms for these problems resonated with the population because it was not widely understood that "many economic developments that happened in the early years of transition had root causes not even in transformation itself, but in over forty years of socialism," writes Marek Tatała. "The reforms freeing the economy and individuals only revealed many failures of the previous system. Hidden unemployment and over-employment or huge inefficiencies, driven by mass state ownership and central planning, were extremely costly. The system was, in fact, dominated by economic lies."[130]

The most important factor was that, beyond the problems that always arise during such a transitional phase, there were also positive impacts that people felt in their everyday lives. Perhaps chief among these was that the product shortages and empty shelves that were so typical of socialist economies were quickly overcome by price reforms and liberalization. Having access to such a wide range of goods convinced many people that the situation was changing for the better.[131]

There was another important factor: the share of employees in the private sector (excluding agriculture) rose from only 13.2 percent in 1989 to 34.4 percent in 1992. Studies have repeatedly shown that employees in the private sector generally offer stronger support to market-economy reforms than employees in state-owned enterprises. In this respect, privatization also had an important political dimension and strengthened the forces of reform.[132]

Every reform produces winners and losers. There are people who quickly adapt to the new conditions and recognize the opportunities of capitalism. They are among those who support the reforms. There are others who cannot or will not adapt as quickly and who benefit less from the reforms.[133] This second group is skeptical of the reforms, and it is this group that is targeted by populists, who know nothing about economics but a lot about how to mobilize people's envy and insecurities.

A new government was formed after the October 1991 elections. Balcerowicz left the government on December 18, 1991 "very tired and with no intention to return."[134] But from 1995, he was chairman of the largest pro-market party in Poland, the Freedom Union, and from October 1997 to December 2000 he again served as Deputy Prime Minister and Minister of Finance.[135] His second term in office was characterized by difficult external conditions, as the Asian and Russian crises shook the financial markets in 1998. During this period, Balcerowicz focused on the following issues:

- Reducing Poland's debt burden.
- Privatization: Most of the banking sector, the large metallurgical sector, telecommunications, and many of the remaining SOEs in manufacturing—but not mining and railways.[136]
- Deregulation: Here he was only partially successful, because the necessary liberalization of the labor market failed due to political resistance.
- Tax reform: His tax reforms, which would have included a flat tax system for income tax, also failed due to political resistance, but some elements of it were later implemented by the former communist party, known at the time as the SLD, and its partners.[137]

In December 2000, Balcerowicz's second term in office came to an end, and from 2001 to 2007 he was governor of the National Bank of Poland. So, were his reforms too radical, as his opponents claim today? Would a slower, more cautious approach have been better? The facts say otherwise, as even Piatkowski admits, despite being more of a social democrat and in no way a staunch pro-capitalist like Balcerowicz. For his part, Balcerowicz believed that the mistakes he made were mostly a result of concession-making and compromise. "All the major errors were errors of omission: the economic team, including the Ministry of Finance, accepted bad proposals from some other ministries, especially the Ministry of Labor, which was in charge of social policies."[138]

For example, his team accepted pensions rising from 43 percent (1989) to 63 percent (1992) of the average wage, which created a significant burden on the pension system. Balcerowicz also later came to believe that there might have been a chance to introduce a flat tax on incomes in 1990, instead of accepting the IMF's proposal for a conventional progressive income tax system, as introduced in 1992. He would also have preferred to see a faster pace in the privatization of the large state-owned enterprises.[139] Despite these self-critical remarks, Balcerowicz's reforms heralded one of the greatest economic successes of the past fifty years, comparable only to the reforms of Margaret Thatcher in Britain, Ronald Reagan in the United States, Deng Xiaoping in China, and the Vietnamese *Doi Moi* reforms launched in the mid-1980s.

Poles Should Not Forget the Reasons for Their Success

However, there is always the danger that people forget the reasons for their prosperity. This is true in many countries today, whether the US, Germany, China, or Chile. This danger also exists in Poland. Although Poland has one of the best and most stable banking systems in the EU, Warsaw has nationalized several banks.[140] And while more than two decades of economic growth in Poland led to a decline in the public debt-to-GDP ratio, in recent years slower growth and increased borrowing have led to a reversal of this trend.[141]

In addition, there are other problems: Poland is among the countries with a serious financial problem in relation to its pay-as-you-go state pension scheme. This is due to Poland's low birth rate, which is below the EU average, and its aging society. It is for this reason that, in 2013, the then ruling PO-PSL coalition (Civic Platform and Polish Peasant's Party), passed a law to successively raise the retirement age to sixty-seven. In the years that followed, the employment rate for both women and men increased significantly.[142] However, the PiS (Law and Justice) party lowered the retirement age again after its election victory in 2015, which will cause significant economic problems for Poland in the medium and long term.[143]

Laszek *et al.* offer the following critique: "In recent years, the Law and Justice party has introduced damaging changes that hit the labor force participation rate of Poles. It reversed a reform introduced by the previous government that raised the retirement age [...]. It introduced many changes that weakened the link between the length of work and contributions and the future pension. In addition to lowering the retirement age, increases in the minimum pension, quota adjustments, pensions for mothers, reductions in contributions for the self-employed, and thirteenth and fourteenth pensions, among others, contributed to this."[144]

The share of state-owned enterprises in Poland, despite all privatization efforts, is still huge compared to other countries. "Despite the remarkable achievements of the Ministry of Property Transformation, or State Property, in the period 1990–2015, the state share in the Polish economy has remained very high. According to figures from the Organization for Economic Cooperation and Development (OECD), Poland ranks first among the OECD's thirty-four member countries in terms of state ownership."[145]

Despite the fact that further significant privatizations would have been necessary, just one year after the PiS party's election victory, the privatization program was essentially halted, and in 2017 the government dissolved the Ministry of State Property. However, the government not only put further privatizations on ice, it launched a new program of nationalizations of previously privatized enterprises. Moreover, there were even attempts to nationalize companies that had always been privately owned.[146]

The Heritage Foundation's *Index of Economic Freedom*, which has already been referred to above, documents the great progress Poland has made in recent decades in comparison with other countries. It nevertheless also highlights the considerable deficits that still exist. Poland is awarded strong ratings in the categories of "investment freedom," "monetary freedom," "trade freedom," "business freedom," and "fiscal health." In contrast, "government spending," "judicial effectiveness," "labor freedom," and "government integrity" are rated very poorly.[147]

Restricting government spending, labor market reforms, and strengthening the rule of law and the independence of the judiciary should be the focus of major reform efforts for Poland. Unfortunately, things have taken a turn for the worse in recent years. This is especially true of the rule of law, which is of great importance for the functioning of a capitalist economic order. A team led by the Polish economist Marek Tatała presented a sobering analysis in 2020 showing how the rule of law—especially the independence of the judiciary—has been increasingly eroded in Poland since 2015. The greatest evil is the politicization of the judiciary. Until 2017, only 32 percent of the members of the National Council of the Judiciary were selected by politicians; after self-described "judicial reforms," the figure was 92 percent.[148] The pretense that the judiciary was riddled with communists is unconvincing, especially considering that the average age of the country's judges was about forty-six. "Moreover, the establishment of the NJC [National Council of the Judiciary] in 1990 and the reform of the SC [Supreme Court] brought about the replacement of over 80 percent of its composition."[149]

The result of the politicization of the judiciary was that Poland lost ground in all major indices that assess the rule of law and democracy, and sparked a serious ongoing conflict with the EU. According to the authors, PiS policies have contributed to the curtailment of economic freedom in Poland. For example, they point to the numerous new regulations that have been introduced, including a ban on the sale of agricultural land, a ban on Sunday shopping, and restrictions on the opening of new pharmacies. In addition, a policy of renationalizing private companies was being implemented. The expansion of state ownership in the banking sector is particularly dangerous for the stability of economic growth, the authors note. They also point out that the Polish state now controls more than 40 percent of banking sector assets after taking over several financial institutions. However, experience shows that state ownership of banks leads to a politicization of their lending policies, for example by subordinating lending decisions to political objectives.[150]

Another issue is the lack of legal certainty, because laws, especially tax laws, are potentially subject to constant changes. "Laws in Poland are changed much more often than in other countries. In the record-breaking year 2016, over 35,000 pages of legislation were passed. Another record was set by the Law and Justice party in 2018, when 362 pages of amendments to tax laws were published. The ruling party's legislative practice was characterized by the extremely hasty enactment of important legislation and a tendency to ignore regular parliamentary procedures, with no obligation to prepare regulatory impact assessments or hold public consultations. In addition, on numerous public infrastructure projects, the government prepared unreliable impact assessments and unjustifiably shortened public consultations, which were, in any case, more of a façade than a real attempt at seeking the public's input. The problem of unpredictability of legislation applies particularly to taxation, where PiS introduced damaging sectoral taxes (especially bank tax and tax on retail trade), additional reliefs (e.g., PIT [personal income tax] exemption for persons under twenty-six years of age, reduced CIT [corporate income tax] for companies with revenues up to EUR 2 million) and de facto additional tax threshold (so-called solidarity surcharge), as well as many other taxes officially called fees (such as emission, recycling, sugar, or power fees). At the same time, the methods used to tighten up the tax system have made it even more repressive."[151]

The PiS party lost its majority following the elections in October 2023 and the country has been governed by a coalition led by Donald Tusk since December 2023. So, we will have to wait and see how Poland's economy develops in the years to come: will the Poles return to the free-market path that has made them so successful in recent decades? Then Poland has a bright future. Or will Poland continue on the path it has taken in recent years, that is, in the direction of more state and less market? That would be tragic, because Poland would lose much of the prosperity it has worked so hard for in the years since 1990.

What People in Poland Think of Capitalism

It is heartening that the majority of Poles still have a positive view of the market economy and capitalism. I commissioned a survey on the image of the market economy and capitalism in thirty-three countries between June 2021 and November 2022. In Poland, Ipsos MORI surveyed a total of 1,096 representatively selected people from July 30 to August 9, 2021, and a total of 33,452 respondents were surveyed in all thirty-three countries.

The survey differs from many other surveys on the market economy and capitalism not only in its depth (i.e., in the level of detail of the questions asked), but also in a particular method: the hypothesis before the survey began was that some people are repelled by the word 'capitalism' in particular, even though their actual views would put them more in the pro-capitalist camp. Thus, one set of questions (on 'Economic Freedom') consistently avoided the word 'capitalism.' Respondents were presented with a total of six statements, of which three statements favored economic freedom and a market economy and three advocated a strong role for the state.

In contrast, the term 'capitalism' was used in the two other sets of questions. First, we wanted to know exactly what the survey's respondents associate with the word 'capitalism,' then we presented each respondent with a total of eighteen statements about capitalism. By combining the data for the last two sets of questions, we are able to determine what people think if the word 'capitalism' is mentioned. It is interesting to compare this with the first set of questions, where the answers reveal how people feel about capitalism when the word is not mentioned. By comparing responses across the three sets of questions, we can see exactly what role the word 'capitalism' plays: in Poland, support for capitalism grows by a massive 122 percent when 'capitalism' is described without using the word.

An analysis of the responses to the pro-state and pro-market statements reveals that statements in favor of a stronger role for the government meet with 15 percent approval, compared with 37 percent approval for pro-market statements in favor of a reduced role for the government. Dividing the average of positive statements by the average of negative statements yields a coefficient of 2.40. I will come back to this coefficient frequently below: a coefficient greater than 1.0 means that pro–economic freedom attitudes dominate; a coefficient less than 1.0 means that anti–economic freedom opinions dominate.

The statement that elicited the greatest agreement by far (46 percent) in Poland was: "I think private businesses alone should decide what products to manufacture and what prices to charge for them; the state should not be involved in that." And the lowest agreement by far (10 percent) was for the statement: "We need a lot more state intervention in the economy, since the market fails time and again" (Figure 4.1).

Figure 4.1 Poland: Six Statements on a Good Economic System

Question: "Below is a list of various things that people have said they consider to be a good economic system. Which of the statements would you say too?"

Note: All data are in percentage of respondents

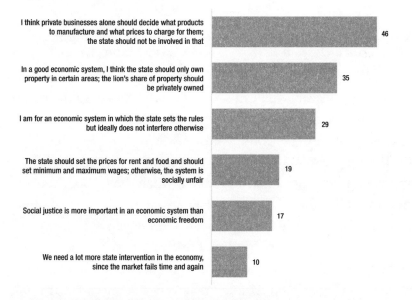

Source: Ipsos MORI survey 20-091774-30

Figure 4.2 Attitudes Toward Economic Freedom in Thirty-Three Countries

Average of statements in favor of a liberal economic system divided by the average of statements in favor of a state-controlled economic system (without using the term 'capitalism')

Note: The lower the coefficient, the stronger the anti-capitalist attitude

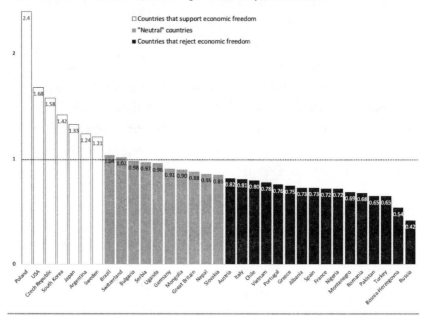

Sources: Allensbach Institute survey 12038, Sant Maral Foundation, Ipsos MORI surveys 20-091774-30, 21-087515-07, 22-014242-04-03 and 22-087515-44, Indochina Research, FACTS Research & Analytics Pvt. Ltd. and Research World International Ltd.

From Figure 4.2, you can see that attitudes toward the market economy were more positive in Poland than in all other countries where the survey was conducted.

The respondents were then presented with ten terms, five positive and five negative, and asked which they associated with the word 'capitalism.' The result: an average of 61 percent of Polish respondents associate 'capitalism' with negative terms such as greed, coldness, and corruption. Positive terms such as prosperity, progress, and freedom, on the other hand, are mentioned by 67 percent (Figure 4.3). Unlike most other countries, our Polish respondents predominantly associate 'capitalism' with positive terms, although it is clear that the level of agreement is lower

Figure 4.3 Poland: Associations with 'Capitalism'

Question: "Please now think about the word capitalism. For each of the following statements, select whether that is something you associate with capitalism."

Note: All data are in percentage of respondents

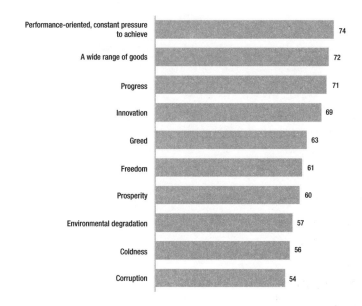

Source: Ipsos MORI survey 20-091774-30

than for the first set of questions on the characteristics of good economic systems, where the term 'capitalism' was not mentioned.

In the next set of questions, respondents were presented with a total of eighteen statements about capitalism, ten of which were negative and eight of which were positive. Agreement with negative statements (averaging 22 percent) and positive statements on capitalism (averaging 23 percent) is finely balanced. Dividing the percentage for the positive statements by the percentage for the negative statements gives us a coefficient of 1.05.

Poland is one of the few countries in which the second-highest-ranked of the eighteen statements on capitalism was

Figure 4.4 Poland: Statements About Capitalism—Ten Negative Statements

Question: "Which of the following statements about capitalism, if any, would you agree with?"
Note: All data are in percentage of respondents

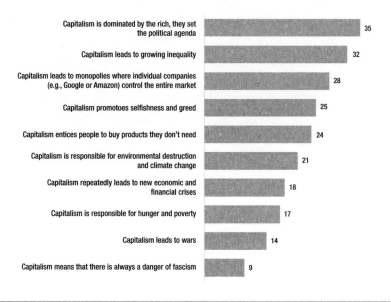

Source: Ipsos MORI survey 20-091774-30

positive: 33 percent of Polish respondents agree that "Capitalism means economic freedom" (Figure 4.5). However, 35 percent of Poles also say "Capitalism is dominated by the rich, they set the political agenda," while 32 percent concur that "Capitalism leads to growing inequality" (Figure 4.4).

At 30 percent, agreement with the statement "Capitalism means that consumers determine what is offered, and not the state" is significantly higher in Poland than in other countries. Presumably because it is something people in other countries take for granted and never even think about, unlike in Poland, where people had got used to living under socialism. Likewise, agreement with the statement "Capitalism may not be ideal, but it is still better than all other economic systems" ranks fifth out of the eighteen statements (29 percent agreement), which can also

Figure 4.5 Statements About Capitalism—Eight Positive Statements

Question: "Which of the following statements about capitalism, if any, would you agree with?"

Note: All data are in percentage of respondents

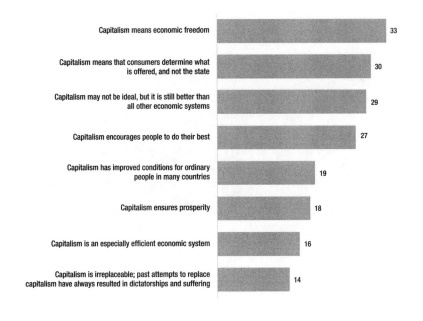

Capitalism means economic freedom	33
Capitalism means that consumers determine what is offered, and not the state	30
Capitalism may not be ideal, but it is still better than all other economic systems	29
Capitalism encourages people to do their best	27
Capitalism has improved conditions for ordinary people in many countries	19
Capitalism ensures prosperity	18
Capitalism is an especially efficient economic system	16
Capitalism is irreplaceable; past attempts to replace capitalism have always resulted in dictatorships and suffering	14

Source: Ipsos MORI survey 20-091774-30

be understood in terms of the historical background of Poland's experience with socialism (Figure 4.5).

In Figure 4.6 you can see that 'capitalism' has a more positive image in Poland, even if the word itself is used, than in all other surveyed countries (combining the figures for economic freedom and the two capitalism questions results in a coefficient of 1.52).

What People in Poland Think of the Rich

In another survey, which I also commissioned, Ipsos MORI collected data to find out what people in different countries think of the rich, and measured the prevalence of social envy in each

Figure 4.6 Overall Coefficient on Attitudes Toward Capitalism in Thirty-Three Countries

Note: The lower the coefficient, the stronger the anti-capitalist attitude

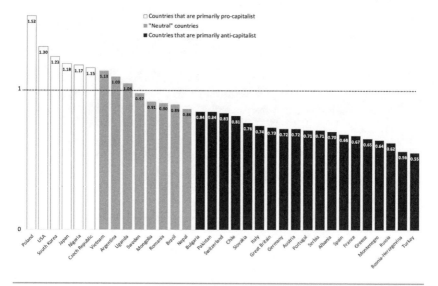

Sources: Allensbach Institute survey 12038, Sant Maral Foundation, Ipsos MORI surveys 20-091774-30, 21-087515-07, 22-014242-04-03 and 22-087515-44, Indochina Research, FACTS Research & Analytics Pvt. Ltd. and Research World International Ltd.

country. The project started in 2018 with surveys in France, Germany, the UK, and the United States, followed by Spain, Italy, Sweden, China, Vietnam, South Korea, and Chile. The survey was conducted in Poland from November 4 to 7, 2022.

The same questions were asked in all countries, with certain adjustments. For example, in countries such as Germany and the United States, we asked questions about "millionaires." We defined "millionaires" as individuals with at least one million euros or dollars in assets (where those are the local currencies) in addition to the home or apartment they use as their main residence. The "one million" figure would not have made sense in countries such as Vietnam or even Sweden where most people would qualify as "millionaires" in the local currency, so we adjusted the sums in those cases. In Poland, we defined the rich as individuals who own assets worth at least four million *zloty* in addition to their primary home. We started by presenting respondents with seventeen statements, both positive and negative, about rich people and asked them whether they agreed or disagreed. The results for Poland are presented in Figure 4.7.

Figure 4.7 Poland: Seventeen Statements About Rich People

Question: "Here is a list of things that people have said about rich people. Which, if any, of the statements on the list would you agree with?"

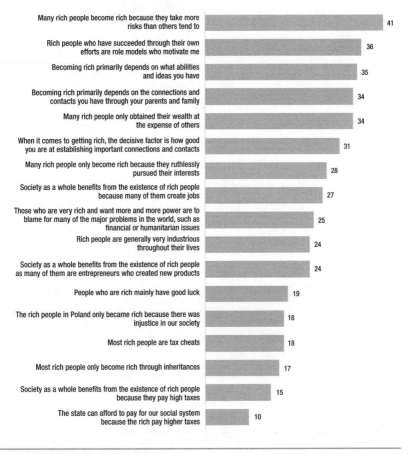

Statement	
Many rich people become rich because they take more risks than others tend to	41
Rich people who have succeeded through their own efforts are role models who motivate me	36
Becoming rich primarily depends on what abilities and ideas you have	35
Becoming rich primarily depends on the connections and contacts you have through your parents and family	34
Many rich people only obtained their wealth at the expense of others	34
When it comes to getting rich, the decisive factor is how good you are at establishing important connections and contacts	31
Many rich people only become rich because they ruthlessly pursued their interests	28
Society as a whole benefits from the existence of rich people because many of them create jobs	27
Those who are very rich and want more and more power are to blame for many of the major problems in the world, such as financial or humanitarian issues	25
Rich people are generally very industrious throughout their lives	24
Society as a whole benefits from the existence of rich people as many of them are entrepreneurs who created new products	24
People who are rich mainly have good luck	19
The rich people in Poland only became rich because there was injustice in our society	18
Most rich people are tax cheats	18
Most rich people only become rich through inheritances	17
Society as a whole benefits from the existence of rich people because they pay high taxes	15
The state can afford to pay for our social system because the rich pay higher taxes	10

Source: Ipsos MORI survey 22-087515-44

Figure 4.8 Greatest Differences between Poland and Germany

Question: "Here is a list of things that people have said about rich people. Which, if any, of the statements on the list would you agree with?"

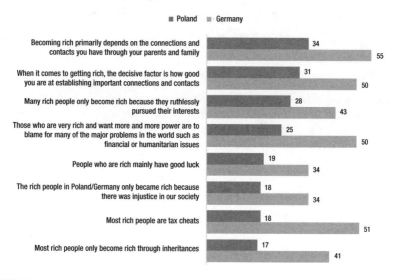

Sources: Ipsos MORI survey 22-087515-44, Allensbach Institute survey 11085

A two-country comparison of results for the same question (Figure 4.8) reveals that people in Poland have a far more positive attitude toward the rich than Germans. For instance, only 18 percent of Poles say that most rich people are tax cheats, compared with 51 percent of German respondents; 25 percent of Poles blame the rich for many of the world's major problems, such as financial or humanitarian issues, while in Germany the figure is twice as high (50 percent).

We also presented respondents with a list of seven positive and seven negative personality traits and asked which of them were most likely to apply to rich people. In Poland, the three most frequently mentioned traits are all positive, namely bold and daring, imaginative, and industrious.

But even the trait mentioned least often is a positive one, namely honesty. When we ask only those Polish respondents

Figure 4.9 Poland: Which Personality Traits Are Most Likely to Apply to Rich People?

Question: "Which, if any, of the following are most likely to apply to rich people?"

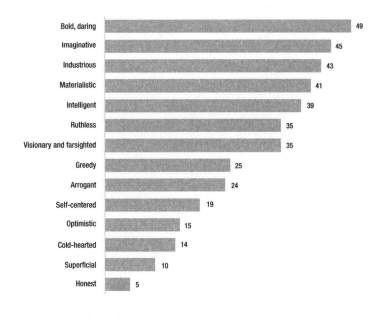

Trait	Value
Bold, daring	49
Imaginative	45
Industrious	43
Materialistic	41
Intelligent	39
Ruthless	35
Visionary and farsighted	35
Greedy	25
Arrogant	24
Self-centered	19
Optimistic	15
Cold-hearted	14
Superficial	10
Honest	5

Source: Ipsos MORI survey 22-087515-44

who personally know one or more rich people which personality traits apply to the rich person they know best, however, there is an interesting difference on the point of "honesty." While only 5 percent of Poles consider rich people in general to be "honest," 20 percent ascribe honesty to the rich person they know personally. It is remarkable that we observe the same trend in all of the countries where we asked this additional question (Figure 4.10).

Despite the differences, there are some points of agreement between our Polish and German respondents. For example, 43 percent of Poles and 42 percent of Germans say rich people are industrious. But it is the differences that are more important. For instance, 19 percent of Poles think the rich are self-centered, in contrast to 62 percent of Germans; 25 percent of Poles, but 49 percent of Germans, think rich people are greedy. And 24 percent

Figure 4.10 Are Rich People Honest?

Question: "Which, if any, of the following are most likely to apply to rich people?" Item chosen: "Honest"

Supplemental question to respondents who personally know a millionaire: "Which, if any, of the following apply to the millionaire you know best?" Percentage of respondents who selected "honest."

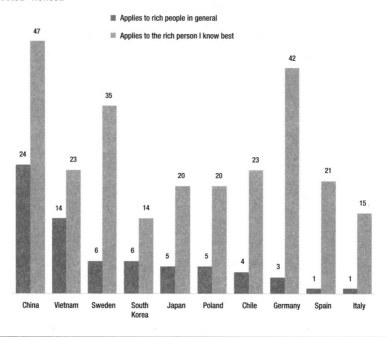

Sources: Allensbacher surveys 11085 and 8271, Ipsos MORI surveys J-18-031911-01-02, J-19-01009-29, J-19-01009-47, J-20-091774-05, and J-21-041026-01

of Poles, compared with 43 percent of Germans, think rich people are arrogant. (Figure 4.11).

When we calculate the average percentage with which Poles attribute positive and negative personality traits to the rich, we arrive at the PTC (Personality Trait Coefficient). A PTC greater than one means that the population of a given country tends to attribute more negative traits to the rich, while a PTC less than one means that respondents are more likely to associate the rich with positive personality traits. Poland has

Figure 4.11 The Personality Traits That People in Poland and Germany Attribute to the Rich

Question: "Which, if any, of the following are most likely to apply to rich people?"

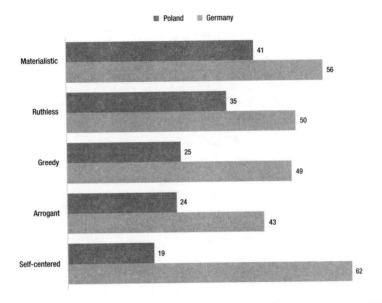

Sources: Ipsos MORI survey 22-087515-44, Allensbach Institute survey 11085

a PTC of 0.7. The only surveyed country in which the population assesses the personality traits of the rich more positively than Poland is Vietnam (Figure 4.12).

The survey contained many other questions, including a number of items that can be considered as indicators of envy. For example, we asked people if they would be in favor of increasing taxes substantially for rich people, even if they would not benefit from it personally. In Poland 44 percent agreed with this statement; in Germany it was 65 percent. One question was used to determine *schadenfreude* and asked respondents what they think when a rich person loses a lot of money through a risky business deal. "It serves him right," say 15 percent of Poles, but 40 percent of Germans. When we

Figure 4.12 International Comparison of the Personality Trait Coefficient PTC

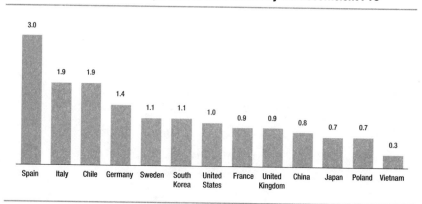

Sources: Allensbach Institute surveys 8271 and 11085, Ipsos MORI surveys 18-031911-01-02, 19-01009-29, 19-01009-47, 20-091774-05, 20-09-1774-30 and 21-041026-01

asked whether Poles would be in favor of drastically reducing the salaries of top-level managers and redistributing the money more evenly among their employees, even when this would mean that they would only get a few more *zloty* per month, only 23 percent of Poles were in favor, but in Germany it was twice as much (46 percent).

Based on the responses to these questions, which were asked in all countries, we calculated what we call the Social Envy Coefficient.[152] This coefficient depicts the ratio of enviers to non-enviers in every surveyed country. In Poland, for example, 13 percent of respondents are social enviers, compared with 61 percent who are non-enviers, resulting in a coefficient of 0.21. In Germany, 33 percent are enviers and 34 percent are non-enviers (SEC = 0.97). The higher the Social Envy Coefficient, the greater the prevalence of social envy in that country. You can see here (Figure 4.13) that in none of the thirteen countries where we conducted the survey is social envy as low as in Poland.

We also asked our Polish respondents which political party they tend to vote for and linked their answers to the other results.

Figure 4.13 International Comparison of the Social Envy Coefficient

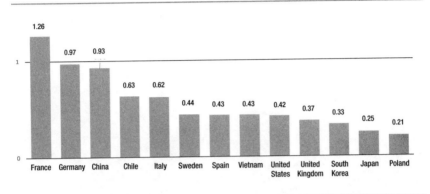

Sources: Allensbach Institute surveys 8271 and 11085, Ipsos MORI surveys 18-031911-01-02, 19-01009-29, 19-01009-47, 20-091774-05, 20-09-1774-30 and 21-041026-01

It is interesting to note the percentage of social enviers among the voters of each party. The proportion of social enviers among all voters in Poland is 13 percent. Of course, there may also be people among the other groups (especially the "ambivalents") who experience social envy. But, according to the hard criteria we apply to our analysis, the figure for Poland is only 13 percent (and thus less than in any other country we have studied).

It is striking that one-in-four supporters (24 percent) of the ex-Prime Minister Jarosław Kaczyński's ruling Law and Justice Party (*Prawo i Sprawiedliwość*—PiS) qualifies as a social envier. So, for this party, pandering to social enviers is a key concern. If the PiS were to lose the support of Poland's social enviers, it would be equivalent to losing a quarter of its voters. Even the "New Left" alliance (*Nowa Lewica*) of Social Democrats (*Sojusz Lewicy Demokratycznej*) and the Green Spring Party (*Wiosna*) do not rely as much on social enviers as the PiS: only 14 percent of their voters are social enviers. The Poland 2050 Party (*Polska 2050 Szymona Hołowni*) also has a 14 percent share of social enviers among its voters. (Figure 4.14).

Figure 4.14 Poland: Social Envy and Voting Preference

Percentage of social enviers among each political party's voters

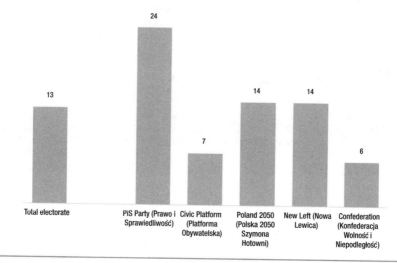

Source: Ipsos MORI survey 22-087515-44

It is not surprising that the PiS attracts more social enviers than any other party. The party is considered "right-wing" or "nationalist-conservative." But while the PiS does hold a number of conservative positions (e.g., on family, migration and nationalism) on the one hand, it is left-wing in terms of its social and economic policies on the other. Social enviers are hardly represented among the voters of Donald Tusk's Civic Platform (*Platforma Obywatelska*), with only 7 percent of this party's voters classed as social enviers. And the Confederation of Freedom and Independence party (*Konfederacja Wolność i Niepodległość*), which unites a peculiar mixture of nationalist, monarchist, and libertarian forces, has only a very small proportion of voters (6 percent) who qualify as social enviers.

In order to measure the overall attitude toward the rich in any given country, we calculated the Rich Sentiment Index (RSI) by combining the Social Envy Coefficient (SEC) and the Personality Trait Coefficient (PTC). With the RSI, coefficients greater

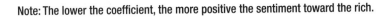

Figure 4.15 International Comparison of the Rich Sentiment Index (RSI)

Note: The lower the coefficient, the more positive the sentiment toward the rich.

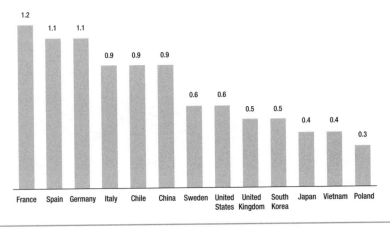

Sources: Allensbach Institute surveys 8271 and 11085, Ipsos MORI surveys 18-031911-01-02, 19-01009-29, 19-01009-47, 20-091774-05, 20-09-1774-30 and 21-041026-01, and Indochina Research

than one mean that attitudes toward the rich are predominantly negative, as in Germany, France, and Spain. The most positive attitudes are in Poland, Japan, and Vietnam. (Figure 4.15).

In many countries, economic upswings followed a change in attitudes toward the rich, such as in China, where Deng Xiaoping proclaimed in the early 1980s that the pursuit of wealth was good, not bad. The same applies to Vietnam and Poland, too, as is evident from the fact that 49 percent of Polish respondents say it is important to them to be or become rich. In the four Asian countries China, Japan, Vietnam, and South Korea the average was even higher, at 58 percent. But in the other European countries and the United States, where our survey was also conducted, an average of just 28 percent agree that it is important to them to become rich. This result thus places Poland closer to the ambitious Asian countries than to Europe and the United States, where people are no longer so ambitious in the pursuit of wealth.

The example of Poland shows how much capitalist reforms can improve the lives of ordinary people in a country, and that sometimes reforms need to be enacted quickly and radically. At such a crucial stage in its history, Poland was fortunate to be led by politicians who were honest and had a clear free-market compass.

CONCLUSION

THE WEALTH AND POVERTY
OF NATIONS

"The definition of insanity is doing the same thing over and over again and expecting different results." This quote is often attributed to Albert Einstein, although there is no irrefutable evidence that he actually said it. But whoever said it, the statement is true. Fifty years of development aid and more than 100 years of experience with socialist experiments have shown that poverty cannot be overcome by redistribution. If Adam Smith could look down on the world today, he would feel vindicated: economic growth conquers poverty; and the prerequisite for economic growth is economic freedom.

In the world of business, companies learn from the best; in business jargon this is aptly called "best practice." Nations can also learn from each other. In this book, I have used the examples of Poland and Vietnam to show how nations can escape poverty. Despite the terrible destruction caused by war and socialism, these countries managed to improve people's living standards year-in year-out over several decades. The recipe was similar in both cases: capitalist reforms. But such reforms cannot simply be imposed from above. In Poland and Vietnam, market-economy structures had already started to develop underground during the socialist period. In Poland, as in all socialist countries, there was a substantial black-market economy without which people would have found it difficult to survive. The black market developed parallel to the official consumer goods market and although such practices were punishable, they were tolerated by the party.

In Vietnam, as in China, informal market structures had already developed before the process of introducing formal reforms began. In part, the reforms only legitimized what had already taken place as spontaneous developments in countless villages. Many agricultural collectives and even state enterprises simply ignored official rules and regulations. They refused to work in collectives and entered into unauthorized contracts ("*khoan chui*") between collectives and families or between state farms and private traders. This practice came to be known as "*pha rao*" ("fence breaking").

Capitalism cannot be imposed from above. The best thing a country's political leadership can do is to refrain from opposing spontaneous developments and create a legal framework for them that provides legal certainty. In both Poland and Vietnam there were countless attempts to improve and "reform" socialism. But by the end of the 1980s at the latest, people realized that it was impossible to implement the necessary reforms from within the system. Vietnam still calls itself a "socialist" country and the governing party calls itself communist. But there are fewer staunch Marxists in Vietnam than in the US or Europe. In Poland, unlike in Vietnam, there was also a break with the old political system.

Besides differences, however, there are far more similarities between these two countries. For example, social envy is not very pronounced in Vietnam or Poland. The Rich Sentiment Index, which I calculated for thirteen countries on the basis of comprehensive surveys, shows that the two countries with the most positive popular opinions of rich people are Poland and Vietnam.[1] The fact that people's views of wealth are not primarily associated with negativity and envy, but that they themselves have the urge to become rich, is a prerequisite for economic dynamism to develop in a country. We asked people in thirteen countries how important it is for them personally to be or become rich. In Germany, 22 percent of respondents said it was important, in the US it was 30 percent, in Poland 49 percent, in China 50 percent, in South Korea 63 percent, and in Vietnam as much as 76 percent.[2]

This book is about nations that have escaped poverty, but it is also worth looking at nations that have made the journey in reverse and fallen into poverty. There is probably no country in the world that has descended so dramatically in the last 100 years as Argentina. In the early twentieth century, the average per capita income of the population was among the highest in the world. The expression *"riche comme un argentin"*—rich as an Argentinean—was a commonly heard expression at the time.[3] Argentina's descent is closely associated with one name: Colonel Juan Domingo Perón. He was elected president in February 1945. His first term lasted until 1955. His political agenda: big government. Argentina's telephone company was nationalized, its railways, its energy supply, its private radio. Between 1946 and 1949 alone, government spending tripled. The number of public-sector employees rose from 243,000 in 1943 to 540,000 in 1955. Many new jobs were created in government agencies and in the civil service to provide for the supporters of Perón's Workers' Party.[4] Economic policy was socialist: although passenger and freight volumes for the railways stagnated, the number of employees increased by more than 50 percent between 1945 and 1955. The Perónist trade unions became the most powerful organizations in Argentina alongside the military. Perón's wife, Eva Duarte, was worshipped like a heroine, dispensing money on social welfare hand over fist. Military dictatorships and Perónist governments replaced each other, and Argentina sank further and further into debt. In 1973, Perón came to power for a third time, and again his agenda consisted of redistribution and strong state regulation. From 1976 to 1983, Argentina was ruled by the military, who brutally persecuted all members of the opposition.

Economically, Argentina's history is one of inflation, hyperinflation, state bankruptcies, and impoverishment. Since its independence in 1816, the country has experienced nine sovereign bankruptcies, the most recent of which was in 2020, a tragic story for such a proud country that was once one of the richest in the world. I have visited Argentina and talked to ordinary people, economists, and politicians. My observation: a growing number of Argentineans realize that the only solution to their problems and a way out of poverty is more capitalism. And that is also why they elected the "anarcho-capitalist" Javier Milei as president in November 2023.

Another woeful example of the decline of a nation is Venezuela. While at the beginning of the twentieth century it was one of the poorest countries in Latin America, by the end of the 1960s Venezuela had undergone a remarkable development. In the course of the last century, Venezuela went from being one of the poorest countries in Latin America to becoming the richest. In 1970, it ranked among the twenty richest countries in the world with a higher per capita GDP than Spain, Greece, and Israel, and only 13 percent lower than that of the UK.[5]

Venezuela's reversal of economic fortune started in the 1970s. One of the reasons for the country's problems was its dependency on its enormous reserves of oil. There were other causes, though, including an unusually high degree of government regulation of the labor market, which was tightened by wave after wave of new regulations from 1974 onward. In hardly any other country in Latin America (or anywhere else in the world, for that matter) was the labor market so heavily regulated. From adding the equivalent of 5.35 months' wages to the cost of employing someone in 1972, non-wage labor costs soared to add the equivalent of 8.98 months' wages in 1992.[6] But, as the example of Venezuela shows, when the problems keep getting bigger, it does not necessarily mean that people will learn. History is not like a Hollywood film with a guaranteed happy ending. Or, to put it another way: things can always get worse.

Many Venezuelans put their faith in the charismatic socialist leader Hugo Chávez as the savior who would deliver their country from corruption, poverty, and economic decline. Chávez was elected president in 1998. A year later, the Republic of Venezuela was renamed the Bolivarian Republic of Venezuela (*República Bolivariana de Venezuela*) at his behest. He was not only a beacon of hope for many of Venezuela's poor; his talk of a new kind of "Socialism for the 21st Century" also reawakened dreams of a utopian paradise among members of the European and North American left. We know how this story ended: Venezuela first lost economic, then political freedom, inflation rose to an absurd 1,000,000 percent, people suffered from hunger, and , to date, 7.5 million Venezuelans have fled the country.

Venezuela's history should be a warning to us: even prosperous, democratic countries are not immune from losing their prosperity and freedom in a matter of just a few years. Freedom, economic as well as political, cannot be taken for granted; it has to be fought for, over and over again. In Poland and Vietnam, too, there is no guarantee that future governments will stick to the path their countries have taken since the late 1980s. Often, after a certain amount of time, people forget why their country has become successful. In Poland today, there is a dangerous tendency toward bigger government and less market. In Vietnam, at least so far, no such tendency has emerged. But without political reforms, it will not ultimately be possible for Vietnam to successfully combat problems such as corruption.

I admire both countries and hope that people in countries that are poor today will take them as an example. I would like to call out to people wherever they are in the world: stop dwelling on the past and looking for culprits in the West. Stop believing that the West can lift you out of poverty with development aid. Study the history of Poland and Vietnam, because that is what holds the key to understanding how nations escape poverty!

BIBLIOGRAPHY

CHAPTER ONE. ADAM SMITH WAS RIGHT:
ONLY ECONOMIC FREEDOM CAN DEFEAT POVERTY

Aslander, Michael S. *Adam Smith zur Einführung*. Hamburg: Junius Verlag, 2007.

Braudel, Fernand. *Civilization and Capitalism, 15th-18th Century*, Vol. I, *The Structures of Everyday Life*. London: William Collins, Sons & Co., 1985.

Deaton, Angus. *The Great Escape: Health, Wealth, and the Origins of Inequality*. Princeton & Oxford: Princeton University Press, 2013.

Fleischacker, Samuel. *Adam Smith*. London & New York: Routledge, 2021.

Gilbert, Geoffrey. "Adam Smith on the Nature of Poverty." *Review of Social Economy* 55, no. 3 (Fall 1997): 273–291.

Hayek, Friedrich August von. *The Constitution of Liberty: The Definitive Edition*. Edited by Ronald Hamowy. London: University of Chicago Press, 2011.

Hayek, Friedrich August von. "Die überschätzte Vernunft." In *Friedrich August von Hayek: Wissenschaftstheorie und Wissen: Aufsätze zur Erkenntnis und Wissenschaftslehre*, edited by Viktor Vanberg, 109–136. Tübingen: Mohr Siebeck, 2007.

Liu, Glory M. *Adam Smith's America: How a Scottish Philosopher Became an Icon of American Capitalism*. Princeton & Oxford: Princeton University Press, 2022.

Marx, Karl. *Capital*, Vol. 1, *A Critique of Political Economy*. London: Penguin Books, 1976.

McCloskey, Deirdre Nansen, & Art Carden. *Leave Me Alone and I'll Make You Rich: How the Bourgeois Deal Enriched the World*. Chicago & London: University of Chicago Press, 2020.

Mises, Ludwig von. *Socialism: An Economic and Sociological Analysis*. Indianapolis: Liberty Fund, 1981.

Norberg, Johan. *Progress: Ten Reasons to Look Forward to the Future*. London: Oneworld Publications, 2017.

Rothbard, Murray N. *Economic Thought Before Adam Smith: An Austrian Perspective on the History of Economic Thought*, Vol. 1. Auburn, AL: Ludwig von Mises Institute, 2006.

Smith, Adam. *Essays on Philosophical Subjects*. Edited by W. P. D. Wightman & J. C. Bryce. Indianapolis: Liberty Fund, 1990.

Smith, Adam. *The Theory of Moral Sentiments*. London: Penguin Group, 2009.

Smith, Adam. *The Wealth of Nations*. London: David Campbell Publishers, 1991.

Streminger, Gerhard. *Adam Smith: Wohlstand und Moral:. Eine Biographie*. Munich: Verlag C.H.Beck, 2017.

Zitelmann, Rainer. *The Power of Capitalism*. London: LID Publishing, 2019.

CHAPTER TWO: WHAT HELPS AGAINST POVERTY— ANDWHAT DOESN'T

Bremer, Frank. *50 Jahre Entwicklungshilfe—50 Jahre Strohfeuer*. Frankfurt: R. G. Fischer Verlag, 2021.

Burnside, Craig, & David Dollar. "Aid, Policies, and Growth." *American Economic Review* 90. no. 4 (September 2000): 847–868. https://www.jstor.org/stable/117311.

Coase, Ronald, & Ning Wang. *How China Became Capitalist*. New York: Palgrave Macmillan, 2012.

Djankov, Simeon, Jose G. Montalvo & Marta Reynal-Querol. "The Curse of Aid." World Bank, April 2005. https://econ-papers.upf.edu/papers/870.pdf.

Dreher, Axel, & Sarah Langlotz. *Aid and Growth: New Evidence Using an Excludable Instrument.* June 2017. http://www.axel-dreher.de/ Dreher%20and%20Langlotz%20Aid%20and%20Growth.pdf.

Easterly, William. "Can Foreign Aid Buy Growth?" *Journal of Economic Perspectives* 17, no 3 (Summer 2003): 23–48.

Easterly, William. "Was Development Assistance a Mistake?" *American Economic Review* 97, no. 2 (May 2007): 328–332.

Easterly, William. *The White Man's Burden: Why the West's Efforts to Aid the Rest Have Done So Much Ill and So Little Good.* Oxford: Oxford University Press, 2006.

Fink, Alexander, und K. Kappner. "Globale Armut: Positive Entwicklung, negative Einschätzung." Institute for Research in Economic and Fiscal Issues, July 3, 2020. https://de.irefeurope. org/Diskussionsbeitrage/Artikel/article/Globale-Armut-Positive-Entwicklung-negative-Einschatzung.

Meegan, Daniel V. "Zero-Sum Bias: Perceived Competition Despite Unlimited Resources." *Frontiers in Psychology* 1 (2010): 191. https:// www.ncbi.nlm.nih.gov/pmc/articles/PMC3153800/.

Moyo, Dambisa. *Dead Aid: Why Aid Is Not Working and How There Is a Better Way for Africa.* New York: Farrar, Straus & Giroux, 2009.

Ovaska, Tomi. "The Failure of Development Aid." *Cato Journal* 23, no. 2 (2003): 175–188.

Paldam, Martin. "The Aid Effectiveness Literature: The Sad Results of 40 Years of Research." *Journal of Economic Surveys* 23, no. 3 (2009): 433–461.

Pinker, Steven. *Enlightenment Now: The Case for Reason, Science, Humanism, and Progress.* New York: Viking, 2018.

Rosling, Hans, with Anna Rosling & Ola Rosling Ronnlund. *Factfulness: Ten Reasons We're Wrong About the World—and Why Things Are Better Than You Think.* London: Sceptre, 2018.

Rubin, Paul H. "Folk Economics." *Southern Economic Journal* 70, no. 1 (2003): 157–171.

World Bank Group, *Poverty and Shared Prosperity 2022: Correcting Course*. Washington, DC, 2002.

CHAPTER THREE: VIETNAM

Altrichter, Helmut. *Kleine Geschichte der Sowjetunion 1917–1991*. 3rd edition. Munich: Verlag C.H.Beck, 2007.

Baum, Anja. "Vietnam's Development Success Story and the Unfinished SDG Agenda." IMF Working Paper No. 2020/031, Asia Pacific Department, February 2020. https://www.imf.org/en/Publications/WP/Issues/2020/02/14/Vietnam-s-Development-Success-Story-and-the-Unfinished-SDG-Agenda-48966.

Beresford, Melanie. "The Development of Commercial Regulation in Vietnam's Market Economy." In *Legal Reforms in China and Vietnam: A Comparison of Asian Communist Regimes*, edited by John Gillespie & Albert H. Y. Chen, 254–268. London & New York: Routledge, 2010.

Boothroyd, Peter, & Pham Xuan Nam, eds. *Socioeconomic Renovation in Viet Nam: The Origin, Evolution, and Impact of Doi Moi*. Singapore & Ottawa: International Development Research Centre Ottawa / Institute of Southeast Asian Studies, 2000.

Bui, Cuong, & Truong Si Anh. "Income-Based Social Stratification in Vietnam 1998–2018." In *Rethinking Asian Capitalism: The Achievements and Challenges of Vietnam Under Doi Moi*, edited by Tran Thi Anh-Dao, 205–219. Cham, Switzerland: Palgrave Macmillan, 2022.

Chu Van Lam, "*Doi Moi* in Vietnamese Agriculture." In *Reinventing Vietnamese Socialism:* Doi Moi *in Comparative Perspective*, edited by William S. Turley & Mark Selden, 151–164. London & New York, Routledge / Taylor & Francis Group, 2019.

Deaton, Angus. *The Great Escape: Health, Wealth, and the Origins of Inequality*. Princeton & Oxford: Princeton University Press, 2013.

Diez, Javier Revilla. "Vietnam Thirty Years After *Doi Moi*: Achievements and Challenges." *Zeitschrift für Wirtschaftsgeographie*

60, no. 3 (January 2016). https://www.researchgate.net/
publication/309449779_Vietnam_30_years_after_Doi_Moi_
Achievements_and_challenges.

Edwards, Vincent, & Anh Phan. *Managers and Management in Vietnam: 25 years of economic renovation* (doi moi). London & New York: Routledge, 2013.

Elliott, David W. P. "Dilemmas of Reform in Vietnam." In *Reinventing Vietnamese Socialism:* Doi Moi *in Comparative Perspective*, edited by William S. Turley & Mark Selden, 53–94. London & New York: Routledge / Taylor & Francis Group, 2019.

Furuta, Motoo. "The Sixth Congress of the Communist Party of Vietnam: A Turning Point in the History of the Vietnamese Communists." In *Indochina in Transition: Confrontation or Co-prosperity*, edited by Mio Tadashi, 1–19. Japan Institute of International Affairs. Tokyo: Toranomon, Minatoku, 1989.

Gillespie, John, & Albert H. Y. Chen, eds. *Legal Reforms in China and Vietnam: A Comparison of Asian Communist Regimes*. London & New York: Routledge, 2010.

Giesenfeld, Gunter. *Land der Reisfelder: Vietnam, Laos und Kambodscha: Geschichte und Gegenwart*. Hamburg: Argument Verlag, 2013.

Glewwe, Paul, Nisha Agrawal & David Dollar, eds. *Economic Growth, Poverty, and Household Welfare in Vietnam*. World Bank Regional and Sectoral Studies. Washington, DC: World Bank, 2004.

Hayton, Bill. *Vietnam: Rising Dragon*. New edition. New Haven & London: Yale University Press, 2020.

Heberer, Thomas. *Private Entrepreneurs in China and Vietnam: Social and Political Functioning of Strategic Groups*. Translated by Timothy J. Gluckman. Leiden & Boston: Brill, 2003.

Ho, Andy, with Joel Weiden. *Crossing the Street: How to Make a Success of Investing in Vietnam*. Petersfield, Hampshire: Harriman House, 2021.

HôChi Minh, "Testament." In *45 Years of President Ho Chi Minh's Testament*. Vietnam Law and Legal Forum, September 29, 2014.

https://vietnamlawmagazine.vn/45-years-of-president-ho-chi-
minhs-testament-4550.html.

Klump, Rainer, and Gerd Mutz, eds. *Doi Moi in Wirtschaft und
Gesellschaft: Soziale und ökonomische Transformation in Vietnam.*
Marburg: Metropolis Verlag, 2002.

Le Ngoc Dang, Dinh Dung Nguyen & Farhad Taghizadeh-Hesary.
"State-Owned Enterprise Reform in Viet Nam: Progress and
Challenges." Working Papers Series No. 1071, Asian Development
Bank Institute, January 2020. https://www.adb.org/publications/
state-owned-enterprisereform-viet-nam-progress-challenges.

Lim, David. *Economic Growth and Employment in Vietnam.* London &
New York: Routledge, 2014.

Lim, Guanie. *The Political Economy of Growth in Vietnam: Between States
and Markets.* New York: Routledge, 2021.

Mai Anh Hoang. *Understanding the Causes of Vietnamese Economic
Growth from 1986 to 2005.* Berlin: regiospectra Verlag, 2011.

Mania, Elodie, Arsene Rieber & Tran Thi Anh-Dao. "Vietnam's
WTO Accession and the Pathway to a Global Field: A Critical
Perspective." In *Rethinking Asian Capitalism: The Achievements and
Challenges of Vietnam Under Doi Moi*, edited by Tran Thi Anh-Dao,
223–250. Cham, Switzerland: Palgrave Macmillan, 2022.

Margara, Andreas. *Der Amerikanische Krieg: Erinnerungskultur in
Vietnam.* Berlin: regiospectra Verlag, 2012.

Mio Tadashi. "Vietnamese Economic Reforms: A Period of Trial
and Error and the Present Situation." In *Indochina in Transition:
Confrontation or Co-prosperity*, edited by Mio Tadashi, 20–56. Japan
Institute of International Affairs. Tokyo: Toranomon, Minatoku,
1989.

Napier, Nancy K., & Dau Thuy Ha. *The Bridge Generation of Vietnam:
Spanning Wartime to Boomtime.* Boise, ID: CCI Press, 2020.

Ngo Vinh Long. "Reform and Rural Development: Impact on Class,
Sectoral, and Regional Inequalities." In *Reinventing Vietnamese*

Socialism: Doi Moi *in Comparative Perspective,* edited by William S. Turley & Mark Selden, 165–207. London & New York: Routledge / Taylor & Francis Group, 2019.

Nguyen, Tam T.T. *Vietnam und sein Transformationsweg: Die Entwicklung seit der Reformpolitik 1986 und aktuelle Herausforderungen.* Hamburg: Diplomica Verlag, 2014.

Nguyen Tri Hung. "The inflation of Vietnam in transition." CAS Discussion Paper No. 22, Centre for ASEAN Studies & Centre for International Management and Development. Antwerp, Belgium, January 1999. https://www.academia.edu/12080147/The_inflation_of_Vietnam_in_transition.

Nguyen Trong Chuan, Nguyen Minh Luan & Le Huu Tang, with Peter Boothroyd & Sharon Manson Singer. "Social Policy." In *Socioeconomic Renovation in Viet Nam: The Origin, Evolution, and Impact of Doi Moi,* edited by Peter Boothroyd & Pham Xuan Nam, 141–172. Singapore & Ottawa: International Development Research Centre Ottawa / Institute of Southeast Asian Studies, 2000.

Nguyen Van Minh. "The Transformation of Mobility in Post–Doi Moi." *Civilisations: Revue internationale d'anthropologie et de sciences humaines,* Special issue, No. 69 (2020) : 128–149. https://journals.openedition.org/civilisations/5770?lang=en.

Opletal, Helmut, ed. *Doi Moi: Aufbruch in Vietnam: Wirtschaftsreform und Nachkriegspolitik.* Frankfurt: Brandes & Apsel Verlag, 1999.

Pfeifer, Claudia. *Konfuzius und Marx am Roten Fluss: Vietnamesische Reformkonzepte nach 1975.* Bad Honnef: Horlemann Verlag, 1991.

Phan Le Ha & Doan Ba Ngoc. *Higher Education in Market-Oriented Socialist Vietnam: New Players, Discourses, and Practices.* Cham, Switzerland: Palgrave Macmillan / Springer Nature, 2020.

Rist, Manfred. "Kriegsheldinnen, Männerersatz und viele Blumen— Vietnam hat gleich zwei Frauentage." *Neue Zürcher Zeitung,* March 8, 2021. https://www.nzz.ch/international/in-vietnam-spielenfrauen-eine-starke-gesellschaftliche-rolle-ld.1605284.

Rushing, Rosanne M., & Charlotte Watts. "The new market economy (Doi Moi) in Viet Nam and its impact on young people." Princeton EU Papers. Undated. https://ipc2005.popconf.org/papers/50294.

Stoffers, Andreas, & Anh Thu Nguyen. *Vietnam und Deutschland: Nachhaltige Entwicklung im Kontext des globalen Wandels: Festschrift zum 45. Jubiläum der deutsch-vietnamesischen Beziehungen.* Hanoi: Verlag der Nationalen Universität von Hanoi, 2019.

Stoffers, Andreas, & Long Quang Pham. *Der aufsteigende Drache: Erfolgreich in Vietnam: Ein interkultureller Guide für alle, die in Vietnam arbeiten oder arbeiten wollen.* Wiesbaden: Springer Gabler, 2021.

Szalontai, Balazs. "The Diplomacy of Economic Reform in Vietnam: The Genesis of *Doi Moi*, 1986–1989." *Journal of Asiatic Studies* 51, no. 2 (June 2008): 199–252. http://www.coldwar.hu/publications/Doi%20Moi%20Article.pdf.

Tarp, Finn. "Vietnam: The dragon that rose from the ashes." WIDER Working Paper 2018/126, United Nations University, World Institute for Development Economic Research (UNU-WIDER), October 2018. https://ideas.repec.org/p/unu/wpaper/wp-2018-126.html.

Tran Thi Anh-Dao. *Rethinking Asian Capitalism: The Achievements and Challenges of Vietnam Under Doi Moi.* Cham, Switzerland: Palgrave Macmillan, 2022.

Tran Thi Que & To Xuan Phuc. "The *Doi Moi* policy and its impact on the poor." In *Social Watch Report 2003: The Poor and the Market*, 182–183. Uruguay, 2003. https://www.socialwatch.org/node/11120.

Turley, William S. "Introduction." In *Reinventing Vietnamese Socialism: Doi Moi in Comparative Perspective*, edited by William S. Turley & Mark Selden, 1–15. London & New York: Routledge / Taylor & Francis Group, 2019.

Turley, William S. "Party, State, and People: Political Structure and Economic Prospects." In *Reinventing Vietnamese Socialism:* Doi Moi *in Comparative Perspective*, edited by William S. Turley & Mark

Selden, 257–276. London & New York: Routledge / Taylor & Francis Group, 2019.

Turley, William S., & Mark Selden, eds. *Reinventing Vietnamese Socialism:* Doi Moi *in Comparative Perspective*. London & New York: Routledge / Taylor & Francis Group, 2019.

Vu Le Thao Chi. *Agent Orange and Rural Development in Post-War Vietnam*. New York: Routledge, 2020.

Weggel, Oskar. "Modernisierungspolitik in Vietnam." In *Doi Moi: Aufbruch in Vietnam: Wirtschaftsreform und Nachkriegspolitik*, edited by Helmut Opletal, 15–28. Frankfurt: Brandes & Apsel Verlag, 1999.

Were, Graeme, "Representing Doi Moi: history, memory and shifting national narratives in late-socialist Vietnam." *International Journal of Heritage Studies*, December 2017. https://www.tandfonline.com/doi/abs/10.1080/13527258.2017.1413677/.

Wolff, Peter. *Vietnam: Die Unvollendete Transformation*. Cologne: Weltforum Verlag, 1997.

Wolz, Axel. "Transformation and Development of Agricultural Co-operatives in Vietnam." In *Doi Moi in Wirtschaft und Gesellschaft: Soziale und ökonomische Transformation in Vietnam*, edited by Rainer Klump & Gerd Mutz, 11–42. Marburg: Metropolis Verlag.

Womack, Brantly. "Political Reform and Political Change in Communist Countries: Implications for Vietnam." In *Reinventing Vietnamese Socialism:* Doi Moi *in Comparative Perspective*, edited by William S. Turley & Mark Selden, 277–305. London & New York: Routledge / Taylor & Francis Group, 2019.

World Bank Group. *From the Last Mile to the Next Mile: 2022 Vietnam Poverty and Equity Assessment*. Washington, DC, 2022. http://hdl.handle.net/10986/37952.

World Bank Group. *Taking Stock, August 2022: Educate to Grow*. Washington, DC, 2002. http://hdl.handle.net/10986/37834.

Wurfel, David. "*Doi Moi* in Comparative Perspective." In *Reinventing Vietnamese Socialism:* Doi Moi *in Comparative Perspective*, edited by William S. Turley & Mark Selden, 19–52. London & New York: Routledge / Taylor & Francis Group, 2019.

Zitelmann, Rainer. "Attitudes towards the rich in China, Japan, South Korea, and Vietnam." *Economic Affairs* 42, issue 2 (June 2022): 210–224. https://onlinelibrary.wiley.com/doi/10.1111/ecaf.12524.

Zitelmann, Rainer. *The Rich in Public Opinion: What We Think About When We Think About Wealth.* Washington, DC: Cato Institute, 2020.

CHAPTER FOUR: POLAND

Aslund, Anders, & Simeon Djankov, eds. *The Great Rebirth: Lessons from the Victory of Capitalism over Communism.* Washington, DC: Peterson Institute for International Economics, 2014.

Balcerowicz, Leszek. *Post-Communist Transition: Some Lessons.* London: Institute of Economic Affairs, 2001.

Balcerowicz, Leszek. *Socialism, Capitalism, Transformation.* Budapest, London & New York: Central European University Press, 1995.

Balcerowicz, Leszek. "Stabilization and Reform under Extraordinary and Normal Politics." In *The Great Rebirth: Lessons from the Victory of Capitalism over Communism*, edited by Anders Aslund & Simeon Djankov, 17–38. Washington, DC: Peterson Institute for International Economics, 2014.

Dudek, Slawomir, & Marcin Zielinski. "More free market or more government? How to strengthen post-pandemic recovery?" FOR Civil Development Forum, Warsaw, 2021.

Filar, Darius. "Rückkehr zum Staatseigentum." Dialog Forum: Perspektiven aus der Mitte Europas, February 2019. https://forumdialog.eu/2019/02/21/rueckkehr-zum-staatseigentum/.

Friszke, Andrzej, & Antoni Dudek. *Geschichte Polens 1939-2015.* Paderborn: Brill Schoningh, 2022.

Gnauck, Gerhard. *Polen verstehen: Geschichte, Politik, Gesellschaft.* Stuttgart: Klett-Cotta, 2018.

Gomulka, Stanislaw. "Poland's Economic Growth in the Global and Long-Term Perspective: Until 2015, The Last Two Years, Forecast." In *Perspectives for Poland: The Polish Economy from 2015–2017 Against the Background of the Previous Years and Future Forecasts*. FOR Civil Development Forum, Warsaw, 2017. https://www.politico.eu/wp-content/uploads/2017/11/Report-Perspectives-for-Poland.-The-Polish-Economy-from-2015%E2%80%932017-Against-the-Background-of-the-Previous-Years-and-Future-Forecasts.pdf.

Havrylyshyn, Oleh, Xiaofan Meng & Marian L. Tupy. "25 Years of Reforms in Ex-Communist Countries: Fast and Extensive Reforms Led to Higher Growth and More Political Freedom." Policy Analysis No. 795, Cato Institute, July 12, 2016. https://www.cato.org/policy-analysis/25-years-reforms-ex-communist-countries-fast-extensive-reforms-led-higher-growth.

Jarosz-Nojszewska, Anna. "Unemployment in Poland in 1918–2018." *Kwartalnik Kolegium Ekonomiczno-Społecznego Studia i Prace* 3:35 (2018): 102–120.

Kaminski, Bartlomiej. *The Collapse of State Socialism: The Case of Poland*. Princeton: Princeton University Press, 1991.

Kienzler, Iwona. *Życie w PRL. I strasznie i śmiesznie*. Warsaw: Bellona, 2015.

Korys, Piotr. *Poland from Partitions to EU Accession: A Modern Economic History, 1772–2004*. London: Palgrave Macmillan, 2018.

Laszek, Aleksander, Rafael Trzeciakowski & Marcin Zielinski. "Poland: Stagnation or Growth? Jobs, the rule of law, investments and innovations." FOR Civil Development Forum, Warsaw, February 2021. https://for.org.pl/en/publications/for-reports/poland-stagnation-or-growth-jobs-the-rule-of-law-investments-and-innovations.

Lenin, Vladimir Ilyich. "The New Economic Policy and the Tasks of the Political Education Departments." In *V. I. Lenin Collected Works*, Vol. 33, *August 1921—March 1923*, 2nd English edition, 60–79. Moscow: Progress Publishers, 1965.

Leszczyńska, Cecylia. *Polska 1918–2018*. Central Statistical Office
of Poland. Warsaw, 2018. https://stat.gov.pl/download/
gfx/portalinformacyjny/pl/defaultaktualnosci/5501/34/1/1/
polska_19182018.pdf.

Lewis, Ben. *Hammer and Tickle: A History of Communism Told Through
Communist Jokes*. London: Phoenix, 2008.

Miller, Terry, Anthony B. Kim & James M. Roberts. *2022 Index
of Economic Freedom*. Heritage Foundation, Washington, DC,
2022. https://www.heritage.org/index/pdf/2022/book/2022_
IndexOfEconomicFreedom_FINAL.pdf.

Mises, Ludwig von. *Socialism: An Economic and Sociological Analysis*.
Indianapolis: Liberty Fund, 1981.

PARP—Polish Agency for Enterprise Development. *Enterprise the
Polish Way*. Polish Agency for Enterprise Development / KARTA
Centre, Warsaw, 2011. https://www.parp.gov.pl/storage/publications/
pdf/2011_enterprise_en.pdf.

Piatkowski, Marcin. *Europe's Growth Champion: Insights from the
Economic Rise of Poland*. Oxford: Oxford University Press, 2018.

Rae, Gavin. *Poland's Return to Capitalism: From the Socialist Bloc to the
European Union*. New York: Palgrave Macmillan, 2018.

Solska, Joanna. *80-te. Jak naprawdę żyliśmy w ostatniej dekadzie PRL*.
Warsaw: Czerwone i Czarne, 2018.

Stodolak, Sebastian. "A Single Law Can Free the Economy. Not for
Long, Though." *Obserwator Finansowy* (Warsaw), December 16,
2013. https://www.obserwatorfinansowy.pl/in-english/a-single-law-
can-free-theeconomy-not-for-long-though/.

Tatała, Marek. "It's Not Only the Economy, Stupid: Progress in Poland
after Socialism." In *Transformative Transformation? 30 Years of
Change in CEE: 4liberty.eu Review* No. 11 (September 2019): 114–127.
https://4liberty.eu/transformative-transformation-30-years-of-
change-in-cee-4liberty-eu-review-no-11-now-available-online/.

Tatała, Marek, Eliza Rutynowska & Patryk Wachowiec. "Rule of Law in

Poland 2020: A Diagnosis of the Deterioration of the Rule of Law from a Comparative Perspective." FOR Civil Development Forum, Warsaw, August 2020. https://for.org.pl/en/publications/for-reports/rule-of-law-in-poland-2020-a-diagnosis-of-the-deterioration-of-the-rule-of-law-from-a-comparative-perspective.

Wojciechowski, Wiktor. "The Labor Market. Impact of Actions after the Elections of 2015: Accelerated Decline in the Workforce." In *Perspectives for Poland: The Polish Economy from 2015–2017 Against the Background of the Previous Years and Future Forecasts.* FOR Civil Development Forum, Warsaw, 2017. https://www.politico.eu/wp-content/uploads/2017/11/Report-Perspectives-for-Poland.-The-Polish-Economy-from-2015%E2%80%932017-Against-the-Background-of-the-Previous-Years-and-Future-Forecasts.pdf.

CHAPTER FIVE: CONCUSION

Bello, Omar, & Adriana Bermudez. "The Incidence of Labor Market Reforms on Employment in the Venezuelan Manufacturing Sector, 1995–2001." In *Venezuela Before Chávez: Anatomy of an Economic Collapse*, edited by Ricardo Hausmann & Francisco Rodriguez, 115–155. University Park: Pennsylvania State University Press, 2014.

Hausmann, Ricardo, & Francisco Rodríguez. "Introduction." In *Venezuela Before Chávez: Anatomy of an Economic Collapse*, edited by Ricardo Hausmann & Francisco Rodríguez, 1–14. University Park: Pennsylvania State University Press, 2014.

Hausmann, Ricardo, & Francisco Rodriguez. "Why Did Venezuelan Growth Collapse?" In *Venezuela Before Chávez: Anatomy of an Economic Collapse*, edited by Ricardo Hausmann & Francisco Rodriguez, 15–50. University Park: Pennsylvania State University Press, 2014.

Riekenberg, Michael. *Kleine Geschichte Argentiniens.* Munich: Verlag C.H.Beck, 2009.

NOTES

CHAPTER 1

1 Smith, *The Theory of Moral Sentiments*, 15.

2 Id. at 13.

3 Streminger, *Adam Smith*, 207.

4 Aßländer, *Adam Smith*, 41; Streminger, *Adam Smith*, 220–221.

5 Smith, *The Wealth of Nations*, 201.

6 Id. at 232.

7 For more on the subject of intellectuals and capitalism, see Zitelmann, *The Power of Capitalism*, chap. 10.

8 Gilbert, "Adam Smith on the Nature and Causes of Poverty," 281.

9 Liu, *Adam Smith's America*, 295 n. 18.

10 Smith, *The Wealth of Nations*, 181.

11 Id. at 465.

12 Id. at 72.

13 Marx, *Capital*, vol. 1, 763.

14 Deaton, *The Great Escape*, 92.

15 McCloskey & Carden, *Leave Me Alone and I'll Make You Rich*, 41.

16 Norberg, *Progress*, 12.

17 Smith, quoted by Dugald Stewart in Smith, *Essays on Philosophical Subjects*, 322.

18 Hayek, *The Constitution of Liberty*, 113.

19 Id. at 112.

20 Smith, *The Wealth of Nations*, 399.

21 Mises, *Socialism*, 357.

22 Hayek, "Die überschätzte Vernunft," 117.

23 Rothbard, *Economic Thought Before Adam Smith*, 435.

24 Id. at 451.

25 Id. at 466.

26 Id. at 468.

27 Fleischacker, *Adam Smith*, 287.

28 Smith, *The Wealth of Nations*, 305.

29 Id. at 306.

CHAPTER 2

1 Bremer, *50 Jahre Entwicklungshilfe*, 7. Several words appear in italics in the original.

2 Id. at 44–45.

3 Id. at 46.

4 Id. at 52.

5 Id. at 83–84.

6 Id. at 62–63.

7 Id. at 64.

8 Easterly, *The White Man's Burden*, 145.

9 Moyo, *Dead Aid*, 36.

10 Bremer, *50 Jahre Entwicklungshilfe*, 75.

11 "630 Millionen Euro: Warum Deutschland Entwicklungshilfe an Weltmacht China zahlt," *FOCUS online*, August 24, 2021, https://www.focus.de/politik/ausland/630-millionen-euro-allein-im-jahr-2017-fast-10-milliarden-euro-seit-1979-darum-zahlt-deutschland-entwicklungshilfe-an-china__id_10817274.html.

12 Cf. Pinker, *Enlightenment Now*, 87; Rosling, *Factfulness*, 52; Fink & Kappner, "Globale Armut: Positive Entwicklung, negative Einschätzung"; and World Bank Group, *Poverty and Shared Prosperity 2022: Correcting Course*.

13 Burnside & Dollar, "Aid, Policies, and Growth."

14 Ovaska, "The Failure of Development Aid," 186.

15 Id. at 187.

16 Easterly, "Can Foreign Aid Buy Growth?" 27.

17 Id. at 30.

18 Id. at 38.

19 Easterly, "Was Development Assistance a Mistake?" 329.

20 Id. at 329.

21 Id. at 330.

22 Id. at 331.

23 Easterly, *The White Man's Burden*, 78.

24 Id. at 88.

25 Id. at 94.

26 Coase & Wang, *How China Became Capitalist*, 49.

27 Paldam, "The Aid Effectiveness Literature," 457.

28 Dreher & Langlotz, *Aid and Growth*, 20.

29 Id. at 20.

30 Djankow, Montalvo & Reynal-Querol, "The Curse of Aid," 1.

31 Meegan, "Zero-Sum Bias," 12.

32 Rubin, "Folk Economics," 157–158.

33 Id. at 158.

34 Cf. id. at 162.

CHAPTER 3

1 Napier & Ha, *The Bridge Generation*, 94.

2 Id. at 96.

3 Id. at 96–97.

4 Id. at 98–99.

5 Id. at 109.

6 Id. at 109.

7 Id. at 110–111.

8 Id. at 125.

9 Id. at 188.

10 Nguyen, Tam T.T., *Vietnam und sein Transformationsweg*, 84–85.

11 Tran Thi Anh-Dao, *Rethinking Asian Capitalism*, 3 n. 1.

12 Mio, "Vietnamese Economic Reforms," 24, tables 1 & 2.

13 Tarp, "Vietnam: The dragon that rose from the ashes," 5.

14 World Bank Group, *From the Last Mile to the Next Mile*, 28, table 1.1.

15 Pfeifer, *Konfuzius und Marx*, 49.

16 "Verluste nach Kriegspartei im Vietnamkrieg 1955–1975," Statista Research Department, last modified August 16, 2023, https://de.statista.com/ statistik/daten/studie/1165881/umfrage/verluste-nach-kriegspartei-im-vietnamkrieg/#:~:text=Im%20Vietnamkrieg%20in%20.

17 Pfeifer, *Konfuzius und Marx*, 49.

18 "Verluste nach Kriegspartei im Vietnamkrieg 1955–1975."

19 Tam T.T. Nguyen, *Vietnam und sein Transformationsweg*, 14.

20 Napier & Ha, *The Bridge Generation*, 120.

21 HôChí Minh, "Testament."

22 Tarp, "Vietnam: The dragon that rose from the ashes," 4 n. 8.

23 Pfeifer, *Konfuzius und Marx*, 60.

24 Id. at 61.

25 Vu Le Thao-Chi, *Agent Orange*, 24.

26 Id. at 24.

27 Id. at 55–56, tables 2.7 & 2.8.

28 Pfeifer, *Konfuzius und Marx*, 61.

29 Id. at 67.

30 Tarp, "Vietnam: The dragon that rose from the ashes," 8.

31 Pfeifer, *Konfuzius*, 72.

32 Id. at 82.

33 Ngo Vinh Long, "Reform and Rural Development," 166.

34 Napier & Ha, *The Bridge Generation*, 126.

35 Tam T.T. Nguyen, *Vietnam und sein Transformationsweg*, 17.

36 Tarp, "Vietnam: The dragon that rose from the ashes," 5.

37 All figures taken from Mai Anh Hoang, *Understanding the Causes*, 23, table 2.1.

38 Chu Van Lam, "*Doi Moi* in Vietnamese Agriculture," 153.

39 Ngo Vinh Long, "Reform and Rural Development," 172.

40 Id. at 176.

41 Altrichter, *Kleine Geschichte der Sowjetunion*, 88.

42 For more background, cf. Geisenfeld, *Land der Reisfelder*, 297 et seq.

43 Pfeifer, *Konfuzius und Marx*, 84.

44 Tarp, "Vietnam: The dragon that rose from the ashes," 22.

45 Nguyen, Tam T.T., *Vietnam und sein Transformationsweg*, 17.

46 Pfeifer, *Konfuzius und Marx*, 86.

47 Mai Anh Hoang, *Understanding the Causes*, 23.

48 Vu Le Thao-Chi, *Agent Orange*, 25.

49 Tran Thi Anh-Dao, *Rethinking Asian Capitalism*, 7.

50 Id. at 8.

51 Mai Anh Hoang, *Understanding the Causes*, 25.

52 Vu Le Thao-Chi, *Agent Orange*, 28.

53 Tam T.T. Nguyen, *Vietnam und sein Transformationsweg*, 20.

54 Wurfel, "*Doi Moi* in Comparative Perspective," 24.

55 Glewwe, Agrawal & Dollar, *Economic Growth, Poverty, and Household Welfare*, 1.

56 Szalontai, "The Diplomacy of Economic Reform in Vietnam," 215.

57 Nguyen Tri Hung, "The inflation of Vietnam in transition," 4, fig. 3.

58 Mio, "Vietnamese Economic Reforms," 32–33.

59 Interview with Nguyen Trong Hoa, November 24, 2022.

60 Id.

61 Interview with Nguyen Quoc Minh-Quang, December 11, 2022.

62 Interview with Vu Dinh Loc, November 29, 2022.

63 Id.

64 Szalontai, "The Diplomacy of Economic Reform in Vietnam," 216.

65 Id. at 212.

66 Mio, "Vietnamese Economic Reforms," 39.

67 Szalontai, "The Diplomacy of Economic Reform in Vietnam," 217.

68 Id. at 220.

69 Furuta, "The Sixth Congress of the Communist Party of Vietnam."

70 Id. at 9–10.

71 Pfeifer, *Konfuzius und Marx*, 98.

72 Id. at 98–99.

73 Quoted in Giesenfeld, *Land der Reisfelder*, 380.

74 Tam T.T. Nguyen, *Vietnam und sein Transformationsweg*, 24.

75 Quoted in Furuta,, "The Sixth Congress of the Communist Party of Vietnam," 15.

76 Id. at 15.

77 Napier & Dau Thuy Ha, *The Bridge Generation*, 198.

78 For more on the following, see Turley, "Introduction," 7.

79 Wurfel, "*Doi Moi* in Comparative Perspective," 32; Turley, "Introduction," 7.

80 Tran Thi Anh-Dao, *Rethinking Asian Capitalism*, 7.

81 Id. at 12.

82 Vu Le Thao Chi, *Agent Orange*, 39, table 2.2.

83 Id. at 39, table 2.2.

84 "Employment in agriculture (% of total employment) (modeled ILO estimate) - Viet Nam" (International Labour Organization, "ILO modelled estimates database" ILOSTAT, accessed January 2021), World Bank, https://data. worldbank.org/indicator/SL.AGR.EMPL.ZS?locations=VN.

85 "GDP contribution of the agriculture, forestry and fishing sector in Vietnam from 2011 to 2022," Statista Research Department, last modified November 7, 2023, https://www.statista.com/statistics/1027971/vietnam-gdp-contribution-of-agriculture-forestry-and-fishing-sector/#:~:text=In%202021%2C%20.

86 Tam T.T. Nguyen, *Vietnam und sein Transformationsweg*, 27–28.

87 Wolz, *Transformation and Development*, 21.

88 Pfeifer, *Konfuzius und Marx*, 106.

89 Id. at 107.

90 Id. at 107.

91 Tam T.T. Nguyen, *Vietnam und sein Transformationsweg*, 45.

92 Id. at 50.

93 Pfeifer, *Konfuzius und Marx*, 114.

94 Tam T.T. Nguyen, *Vietnam und sein Transformationsweg*, 51.

95 Id. at 50.

96 Pfeifer, *Konfuzius und Marx*, 114–115.

97 Tam T.T. Nguyen, *Vietnam und sein Transformationsweg*, 34.

98 Hayton, *Vietnam: Rising Dragon*, 8–9.

99 Furuta, "The Sixth Congress of the Communist Party of Vietnam," 16.

100 Id. at 16.

101 Id. at 16.

102 Interview with Lam Duc Hung, December 14, 2022.

103 Turley, "Introduction," 8.

104 Tam T.T. Nguyen, *Vietnam und sein Transformationsweg*, 54–55.

105 Mania, Rieber & Tran Thi Anh-Dao, "Vietnam's WTO Accession,"225.

106 "The U.S.-Vietnam Bilateral Trade Agreement (BTA)," U.S. Embassy & Consulate in Vietnam, accessed December 12, 2023, https://vn.usembassy.gov/ the-u-s-vietnam-bilateral-trade-agreement-bta-resources-for-understanding.

107 "Handel zwischen Vietnam und den USA nach zehn Jahren Handelsabkommen," VOVWorld, last modified December 14, 2011, https://

vovworld.vn/de-DE/politische-aktualitat/handel-zwischen-vietnam-und-den-usa-nach-zehn-jahren-handelsabkommen-61686.vov.

108 Mania, Rieber & Tran Thi Anh-Dao, "Vietnam's WTO Accession," 245.

109 Id. at 225.

110 Ho, *Crossing the Street*, 17.

111 Id. at 8.

112 Id. at 8.

113 Cf. Mai Anh Hoang, *Understanding the Causes*, 116.

114 Id. at 125.

115 Id. at 124.

116 U.S. Department of State, "2022 Investment Climate Statements: Vietnam," accessed December 12, 2023, https://www.state.gov/reports/2022-investment-climate-statements/vietnam/.

117 World Bank Group, *From the Last Mile to the Next Mile*, 58.

118 Id. at 58.

119 Interview with Vu Dinh Loc, November 29, 2022.

120 Interview with Nguyen Trong Hoa, November 24, 2022.

121 Interview with Nguyen Thi Quat, December 5, 2022.

122 Interview with Nguyen Quoc Minh-Quang, December 11, 2022.

123 Mai Anh Hoang, *Understanding the Causes*, 30.

124 Id. at 33.

125 World Bank Group, *From the Last Mile to the Next Mile*, 28, table 1.1.

126 Id. at 28, table 1.1.

127 René Muschter, "Vietnam: Lebenserwartung bei der Geburt aufgeschlüsselt nach Geschlecht von 1950 bis 2022 und Prognosen bis 2050," Statista, last modified January 12, 2023, https://de.statista.com/statistik/daten/studie/751227/umfrage/lebenserwartung-in-vietnam/#:~:text=Im%20Jahr%202021%20betrug%20die.

128 "Vietnam: Human development," The Global Economy, accessed December 12, 2023, https://www.theglobaleconomy.com/Vietnam/human_development/.

129 Id.

130 World Bank Group, *From the Last Mile to the Next Mile*, 4.

131 Id. at 4.

132 Id. at 8.

133 Bui & Truong Si Anh, "Income-Based Social Stratification in Vietnam," 210, table 9.1.

134 Deaton, *The Great Escape*, 89.

135 The Cuong Bui & Si Anh Truong, "Income-Based Social Stratification in Vietnam," 212, table 9.2.

136 World Bank Group, *From the Last Mile to the Next Mile*, 42.

137 Nguyen Trong Chuan, Nguyen Minh Luan & Le Huu Tang, "Social Policy," 153.

138 Id. at 153.

139 Id. at 153.

140 Id. at 157.

141 Id. at 158.

142 Id. at 158.

143 Id. at 155 n. 23.

144 Id. at 158.

145 World Bank Group, *From the Last Mile to the Next Mile*, 39, table 1.5.

146 Houtart, quoted in Giesenfeld, *Land der Reisfelder*, 389.

147 Id. at 390.

148 Zitelmann, "Attitudes towards the rich."

149 "Frauen in Führungspositionen in der EU," Statistiches Bundesamt (Destatis), accessed December 12, 2023, https://www.destatis.de/Europa/DE/Thema/Bevoelkerung-Arbeit-Soziales/Arbeitsmarkt/Qualitaet-der-Arbeit/_dimension-1/08_frauen-fuehrungspositionen.html#:~:text=Lettland%20war%20mit%20einem%20.

150 Rist, "Kriegsheldinnen, Männerersatz und viele Blumen."

151 "How a Vietnamese Businesswoman Became a Billionaire Thanks to Bikinis," *Fortune*, April 14, 2017, https://fortune.com/2017/04/14/vietjet-bikini-billionaire/.

152 "Nguyen Thi Phuong Thao takes VietJet from 'bikini flights' to IPO in 5 years," CNBC, updated May 25, 2016, https://www.cnbc.com/2016/05/24/nguyen-thi-phuong-thao-takes-vietjet-from-bikini-flights-to-ipo-in-5-years.html.

153 Ho, *Crossing the Street*, 104.

154 Id. at 107.

155 Id. at 101.

156 Id. at 107.

157 Le Ngoc Dang, Dinh Dung Nguyen & Taghizadeh-Hesary, "State-Owned Enterprise Reform in Viet Nam," 2.

158 Id. at 2.

159 Id. at 3.

160 Id. at 2.

161 Id. at 4, table 2.

162 Id. at 6, fig. 4.

163 Id. at 8, table 3.

164 Beresford, "The Development of Commercial Regulation," 263.

165 Ho, *Crossing the Street*, 43.

166 Beresford, "The Development of Commercial Regulation," 263.

167 "Beschleunigung der Privatisierung staatlicher Unternehmen," VOVWorld, November 23, 2018, https://vovworld.vn/de-DE/politische-aktualitat/ beschleunigung-der-privatisierung-staatlicher-unternehmen-701892.vov.

168 Beresford, "The Development of Commercial Regulation," 260.

169 Id. at 261.

170 Id. at 264.

171 Id. at 262.

172 "Korruption in Vietnam," Laenderdaten.info, accessed December 12, 2023, https://www.laenderdaten.info/Asien/Vietnam/korruption.php.

173 Ha Linh Bui, "Videoüberwachung und Todesstrafen: Vietnams Kampf gegen die Korruption," Friedrich Naumann Stiftung, July 22, 2020, https://www. freiheit.org/de/videoueberwachung-und-todesstrafen-vietnams-kampf-gegen-die-korruption.

174 Id.

175 Womack, "Political Reform and Political Change," 282.

176 Wurfel, "*Doi Moi* in Comparative Perspective," 19.

177 Turley, "Party, State, and People," 265.

178 Id. at 266.

179 Szalontai, "The Diplomacy of Economic Reform in Vietnam," 241–242.

180 Id. at 212.

181 Elliott, "Dilemmas of Reform in Vietnam," 73.

182 Wurfel, "*Doi Moi* in Comparative Perspective," 20.

183 Turley, "Party, State, and People," 259.

184 Id. at 259.

185 Id. at 263.

186 Id. at 263.

187 Wurfel, "*Doi Moi* in Comparative Perspective," 46.

188 Id. at 38

189 Id. at 38–39.

190 Turley, "Introduction," 8.

191 Wurfel, "*Doi Moi* in Comparative Perspective," 41.

192 Id. at 34–35.

193 Turley, "Party, State, and People," 272.

194 Kat Devlin, "40 years after fall of Saigon, Vietnamese see U.S. as key ally," Pew Research Center, April 30, 2016, https://www.pewresearch.org/short-reads/2015/04/30/vietnamese-see-u-s-as-key-ally/.

195 Margara, *Der amerikanische Krieg*, 54.

196 Vu Le Thao Chi, *Agent Orange*, 7.

197 Margara, *Der amerikanische Krieg*.

198 Id. at 101–102.

199 Napier & Dau Thuy Ha, *The Bridge Generation*, 213–214.

200 In EU countries and the US, the survey used the term "millionaire." This would not have made sense in Vietnam as, given the currency, practically everyone is a millionaire. Ten billion đồng is equivalent to only €400,000 (not the amount of €1 million used in the survey in Europe), but a somewhat lower number was chosen in Vietnam as it better suits local conditions. The point here was not an exact sum, but that the respondents associate a similar idea with what is meant by the term "rich."

CHAPTER 4

1 Kienzler, *Życie w PRL. I strasznie i śmiesznie*, 300.

2 Solska, *80-te. Jak naprawdę żyliśmy w ostatniej dekadzie PRL*, 52.

3 Lewis, *Hammer and Tickle*, 210.

4 "GDP per capita (constant LCU) – Poland," World Bank, accessed December 12, 2023, https://data.worldbank.org/indicator/NY.GDP.PCAP. KN?locations=PL.

5 Ralf Mielke, "Im Wirtschaftswunderland," Deutsche Bank, accessed December 12, 2023, https://www.deutsche-bank.de/ms/results-finanzwissen-fuer-unternehmen/international/01-2020_im-wirtschaftswunderland. html; and Bruno Urmersbach, "Europäische Union: Einwohnerzahl in den EU-Mitgliedstaaten im Jahr 2023 und Prognosen bis zum Jahr 2100," Statista, September 5, 2023, https://de.statista.com/statistik/daten/studie/164004/ umfrage/prognostizierte-bevoelkerungsentwicklung-in-den-laendern-der-eu/.

6 Miller, Kim & Roberts, *2022 Index of Economic Freedom*, Heritage Foundation.

7 Id. at 452–454.

8 Prof. Dr. Stefan Garsztecki, "Analyse: Deutsche Kriegsreparationen an Polen? Hintergründe und Einschätzungen eines nicht nur innerpolnischen Streites," Bundszentrale für politische Bildung, November 27, 2018, https:// www.bpb.de/themen/europa/polen-analysen/281439/analyse-deutsche-kriegsreparationen-an-polen-hintergruende-und-einschaetzungen-eines-nicht-nur-innerpolnischen-streites/.

9 Information from the "Faces of Totalitarianism" exhibition of the Karta Archive in Poland: "Soviet repression after 1939."

10 Gnauck, *Polen verstehen*, 101.

11 Id. at 102.

12 Korys, *Poland from Partitions to EU Accession*, 287–288.

13 Friszke & Dudek, *Geschichte Polens*, 179.

14 Korys, *Poland from Partitions to EU Accession*, 267.

15 Friszke & Dudek, *Geschichte Polens*, 187.

16 Id. at 188.

17 Id. at 197.

18 Korys, *Poland from Partitions to EU Accession*, 268.

19 Id. at 295.

20 Piatkowski, *Europe's Growth Champion*, 88, table 3.1.

21 Id. at 89.

22 Id. at 90.

23 Id. at 90.

24 Id. at 90–91.

25 Friszke & Dudek, 204.

26 Id. at 205.

27 Id. at 220.

28 Id. at 221.

29 "Inicjatywa na marginesie," Karta Nr. 26, 1998, Report from Kraków, July 1950, in PARP, *Enterprise the Polish Way*, 26.

30 Friszke & Dudek, *Geschichte Polens*, 244.

31 Id. at 268.

32 Id. at 282.

33 Id. at 286.

34 Rae, *Poland's Return to Capitalism*, 45.

35 Friszke & Dudek, *Geschichte Polens*, 391.

36 Kienzler, *Życie w PRL. I strasznie i śmiesznie*, 55.

37 Solska, *80-te. Jak naprawdę żyliśmy w ostatniej dekadzie PRL*, 136.

38 Id. at 117.

39 Id. at 53.

40 Wojciech Oleksiak, "10 Mind-Boggling Oddities of Poland Under the Communist Regime: 9. You needed to wait 20 years to have a phone installed," Culture.pl, accessed December 12, 2023, https://culture.pl/en/article/10-mind-boggling-oddities-of-poland-under-the-communist-regime.

41 Leszczyńska, *Polska 1918–2018* (Central Statistical Office of Poland), 272

42 *Statistisches Jahrbuch 1990 für die Bundesrepublik Deutschland; Statistisches Jahrbuch 1991 für das vereinigte Deutschland; Sozialreport 1990 (Daten und Fakten zur sozialen Lage in der DDR); Datenreport 2008.*

43 Leszczyńska, *Polska 1918–2018.*

44 *Statistisches Jahrbuch 1990 für die Bundesrepublik Deutschland.*

45 Mieczyslaw F. Rakowski, *Dzienniki polityczne 1972–1975* (Warsaw, 2002), quoted in PARP, *Enterprise the Polish Way*, 32. The original Polish to English translation has been modified to make it read more easily.

46 Korys, *Poland from Partitions to EU Accession*, 294. The original Polish to English translation has been modified to make it read more easily.

47 Kienzler, *Życie w PRL. I strasznie i śmiesznie*, 136–137.

48 "Pan Krzysio i handel zagraniczny," Wprost Nr. 27/1986, in PARP, *Enterprise the Polish Way*, 39. The original Polish to English translation has been modified to make it read more easily.

49 "the christmas tale of food polka. oranges and irony," foodpolka.com, December 24, 2013, https://foodpolka.com/2013/12/24/the-christmas-tale-of-food-polka-oranges-and-irony/.

50 Kaminski, *The Collapse of State Socialism*, 51.

51 Id. at 52.

52 Id. at 73.

53 Id. at 73.

54 For more details, cf. Korys, *Poland from Partitions to EU Accession*, 278 et seq.

55 Rae, *Poland's Return to Capitalism*, 49, 53.

56 Id. at 54.

57 Piatkowski, *Europe's Growth Champion*, 125.

58 Id. at 126.

59 Id. at 126.

60 Id. at 127.

61 Id. at 127.

62 Friszke & Dudek, *Geschichte Polens*, 326

63 Id. at 329.

64 Id. at 417.

65 Stodolak, "A Single Law Can Free the Economy," unnumbered.

66 Lenin, "The New Economic Policy," 63.

67 Id. at 64.

68 Baberowski, *Scorched Earth*, 68.

69 *Journal of Laws of the Republic of Poland*, No. 109/2000, quoted in PARP, *Enterprise the Polish Way*, 40.

70 Leszek Kostrzewski & Piotr Miaczynski, *20 lat minelo* (Warsaw, 2009), quoted in PARP, *Enterprise the Polish Way*, 41.

71 Stodolak, "A Single Law Can Free the Economy," unnumbered.

72 Balcerowicz, "Stabilization and Reforms," 19.

73 Id. at 20.

74 Rae, *Poland's Return to Capitalism*, 48.

75 Piatkowski, *Europe's Growth Champion*, 93.

76 Balcerowicz, *Socialism, Capitalism, Transformation*, 315, table 16.1.

77 Id. at 316.

78 Id. at 307.

79 Id. at 323–324.

80 Id. at 324.

81 Rae, *Poland's Return to Capitalism*, 56.

82 Balcerowicz, *Socialism, Capitalism, Transformation*, 325, table 16.2.

83 Rae, *Poland's Return to Capitalism*, 61.

84 Balcerowicz, *Socialism, Capitalism, Transformation*, 323.

85 Piatkowski, *Europe's Growth Champion*, 169; for long-term unemployment, cf. Rae, *Poland's Return to Capitalism*, 64, table 3.5.

86 "Wirtschaft im Sozialismus: Wie die DDR Arbeitslose versteckte," News. de, May 20, 2009, https://www.news.de/wirtschaft/834923025/wirtschaft-im-sozialismus-wie-die-ddr-arbeitslose-versteckte/1/.

87 Ewa Zjawiona, "Kształtowanie się rynku pracy w Polsce przed i po przekształceniach systemowych," *Studenckie Prace Prawnicze, Administratywistyczne i Ekonomiczne* 2 (2004): 99–111, https://www. repozytorium.uni.wroc.pl/Content/34836/PDF/009.pdf.

88 Barbara Brylska, "Aktywna polityka rynku pracy w Polsce," *Annales Universitatis Mariae Curie-Skłodowska, Sectio H, Oeconomia* 31 (1997): 1–14, https://bazhum.muzhp.pl/media/files/Annales_Universitatis_Mariae_ Curie_Sklodowska_Sectio_H_Oeconomia/Annales_Universitatis_ Mariae_Curie_Sklodowska_Sectio_H_Oeconomia-r1997-t31/ Annales_Universitatis_Mariae_Curie_Sklodowska_Sectio_H_ Oeconomia-r1997-t31-s1-14/Annales_Universitatis_Mariae_Curie_ Sklodowska_Sectio_H_Oeconomia-r1997-t31-s1-14.pdf

89 Jarosz-Nojszewska, "Unemployment in Poland in 1918–2018."

90 Kienzler, *Życie w PRL. I strasznie i śmiesznie*, 244.

91 Lewis, *Hammer and Tickle*, 291. The original Polish to English translation has been modified to make it read more easily.

92 Balcerowicz, *Socialism, Capitalism, Transformation*, 328.

93 Id. at 328.

94 Id. at 329.

95 In *Kobieta i zycie* Nr. 42/1990, quoted in PARP, *Enterprise the Polish Way*, 46. The original Polish to English translation has been modified to make it read more easily.

96 *Cash* No 22/1993, quoted in PARP, *Enterprise the Polish Way*, 78.

97 Balcerowicz, *Socialism, Capitalism, Transformation*, 329.

98 Id. at 333.

99 All data is taken from Balcerowicz, *Socialism, Capitalism, Transformation*, 334, table 16.3.

100 Piatkowski, *Europe's Growth Champion*, 127.

101 Gomulka, "Poland's Economic Growth," unnumbered.

102 Piatkowski, *Europe's Growth Champion*, 114–115.

103 Id. at 128.

104 Id. at 130.

105 Id. at 131.

106 Id. at 139.

107 Id. at 146.

108 Balcerowicz, *Socialism, Capitalism, Transformation*, 333.

109 Adriana Sas, "Number of deaths attributable to air pollution in Poland from 1990 to 2019," Statista, January 13, 2022, https://www.statista.com/ statistics/827777/air-pollution-deaths-poland/.

110 Piatkowski, *Europe's Growth Champion*, 147–148.

111 Tatała, "It's Not Only the Economy, Stupid," 122.

112 "CO_2 emissions (metric tons per capita) – Poland," World Bank, accessed December 12, 2023, https://data.worldbank.org/indicator/EN.ATM.CO2E. PC?locations=PL.

113 Piatkowski, *Europe's Growth Champion*, 150.

114 "Polen: Lebenserwartung bei der Geburt, gesamt (Jahre)," Tilasto, accessed December 12, 2023, https://www.tilasto.com/land/polen/bevoelkerung-und-gesundheit/lebenserwartung-bei-der-geburt-gesamt.

115 Piatkowski, *Europe's Growth Champion*, 260.

116 Balcerowicz, "Stabilization and Reforms," 25.

117 Id. at 24.

118 Piatkowski, *Europe's Growth Champion*, 167.

119 Id. at 167.

120 Id. at 171.

121 Havrylyshyn, Meng & Tupy, "25 Years of Reforms," 1.

122 Id. at 13–14.

123 Id. at 17.

124 Cf. id. at 15.

125 Id. at 22.

126 Balcerowicz, *Post-Communist Transition*, 18.

127 Id. at 49.

128 Balcerowicz, "Stabilization and Reforms," 27.

129 Balcerowicz, *Socialism, Capitalism, Transformation*, 309.

130 Tatała, "It's Not Only the Economy, Stupid," 117.

131 Balcerowicz, *Socialism, Capitalism, Transformation*, 308.

132 Id. at 308.

133 Id. at 263.

134 Balcerowicz, "Stabilization and Reforms," 27.

135 Dates from id. at 17.

136 Id. at 34.

137 Id. at 35.

138 Id. at 28.

139 Id. at 28.

140 Dudek & Zielinski, "More free market or more government?" 7.

141 Id. at 7–8.

142 Wojciechowski, "The Labor Market," unnumbered.

143 Id.

144 Laszek, Trzeciakowski & Zielinski, "Poland: Stagnation or Growth?" 4.

145 Filar, "Rückkehr Staatseigentum."

146 "Poland," *2022 Index of Economic Freedom*, Heritage Foundation, February 14, 2022, https://www.heritage.org/index/pdf/2022/countries/2022_IndexofEconomicFreedom-Poland.pdf.

147 Id.

148 Tatała, Rutynowska & Wachowiec, "Rule of Law in Poland 2020," 18.

149 Id. at 14.

150 Laszek, Trzeciakowski & Zielinski, "Poland: Stagnation or Growth?" 5.

151 Id. at 5.

152 For the exact calculation method, cf. Zitelmann, *The Rich in Public Opinion*, 160 et seq.

CONCLUSION

1 See Figure 3.10 on page 99.

2 See Figure 3.3 on page 93.

3 Rieckenberg, *Geschichte Argentiniens*, 110.

4 Id. at 148–149.

5 Hausmann & Rodríguez, "Introduction," 1.

6 Bello & Bermúdez, "The Incidence of Labor Market Reforms," 117.

INDEX OF PERSONS